The fine essays in *The Grace of Grass and Water: Writing in Honor of Paul Gruchow* offer personal recollections and reflections about Paul Gruchow's life, and, a sense, from his peers, of his vital contribution to the literature of place. The inclusion of Paul Gruchow's own essay "The Meaning of Natural History" is sufficient reason to own the book. The essay, here published for the general reader for the first time, is a history of the greats of American nature writing. It offers readers a superb overview of the growth of a field, as well as insights into why, now more than ever, we must understand the earth in order to save it.

 —Emilie Buchwald, publisher emeritus, Milkweed
 Editions; publisher, The Gryphon Press

This elegantly produced collection of memorial essays is a treasure not only for those who cherished Paul Gruchow as a lyric essayist and fond friend but as a clarion voice for political courage. Paul and I were kids together—working on the student paper at the University, pretending our way into being writers. As the decades passed it seemed he was always there, saying the right thing at the right moment. And then, shockingly, he wasn't there. It's still a signal loss, and this book of essays by some of our best essayists and poets goes a long way toward reminding us of his charm and his fierce courage, and especially his enduring hopes for the planet.

 —Patricia Hampl, author, *Blue Arabesque: A Search*
 for the Sublime

Beloved in his home place, Paul Gruchow deserves to be known far and wide, and this lovely volume makes clear exactly why.

 —Bill McKibben, author, *Deep Economy: The*
 Wealth of Communities and the Durable Future

A useful introduction to Gruchow's work and a lovely tribute to his life. Its reminiscences, appreciations, and analyses are as eloquent and insightful as the books of the man it honors.

—David Pichaske, author, *Rooted: Seven Midwest Writers of Place*

As these essays reveal, Paul Gruchow was a brilliant writer and a profound thinker who never failed to amaze his friends and acquaintances with his wisdom and kindness. Gruchow's work—like his life—resonates with passion and intensity. Whether writing about the Boundary Waters of Minnesota, the Beartooth Range of Montana or the Sandhill Cranes of Nebraska, Gruchow makes us see, think and feel in new ways and, ultimately, gaze inward to confront the hard, painful questions of our own humanity—something that Gruchow knew all too well in his own tragic life. He was our generation's Thoreau. *The Grace of Grass and Water* is a deeply moving and fitting tribute to the man and his work.

—Thom Tammaro, coeditor, *Imagining Home: Writing from the Midwest* and *Inheriting the Land: Contemporary Voices from the Midwest*

We are fortunate Paul Gruchow was a writer, for American stands in dire need of his vision and understanding. This collection of beautiful essays will serve as an invaluable introduction to the complicated life of a true American hero.

—Paul Theobald, author, *Teaching the Commons: Place, Pride, and the Renewal of Community*

The Grace of Grass and Water

Writing in Honor of Paul Gruchow

Bob Artley Carol Bly
Thomas Dean Gary Deason
Paul Gruchow Jim Heynen
Bill Holm Louis Martinelli
Mary Pipher Mark Vinz

The Ice Cube Press
North Liberty, Iowa USA

The Grace of Grass and Water
Writing in Honor of Paul Gruchow
Editor, Thomas K. Dean

ISBN 1-888160-28-4 (9781888160284)

Library of Congress Control Number: 2006936768

Ice Cube Press (est. 1993)
205 North Front Street
North Liberty, Iowa 52317-9302
www.icecubepress.com

Manufactured in the United States of America.

The paper used in this publication meets the minimum requirements of the American National Standard for Information Sciences—Permanence of Paper for Printed Library Materials, ANSI Z39.48-1992

Thanks go to Sarah T. (Sally) Williams, Gene Bakko, as well as Jack & Anne Ozegovic for vital help in this book's creation.

Permission to reprint "The Meaning of Natural History" by Paul Gruchow granted by Louis Martinelli.

Cover photos courtesy of Thomas K. Dean, front bottom (Sundew Pond, Superior National Forest) and John Gregor, front top (Aspen Tallgrass Prairie), and back (prairie road, Felton Prairie).

Books by Paul Gruchow (in chronological order)

Journal of a Prairie Year. Minneapolis: University of Minnesota Press, 1985.

The Necessity of Empty Places. New York: St. Martin's Press, 1988. Rpt. Minneapolis: Milkweed Editions, 1999, with a new preface by Gruchow.

Travels in Canoe Country. Photographs by Gerald Brimacombe. Boston: Little, Brown and Company, 1992.

Grass Roots: The Universe of Home. Minneapolis: Milkweed Editions, 1995.

Boundary Waters: The Grace of the Wild. Minneapolis: Milkweed Editions, 1997.

Worlds within a World: Reflections on Visits to Minnesota Scientific and Natural Area Preserves. St. Paul: Minnesota Department of Natural Resources, 1999.

Photograph courtesy of John Gregor

Paul Gruchow was raised on a small subsistence farm near
Montevideo, Minnesota. He is the author of six published books
on subjects ranging from the culture of the tallgrass prairie to
what we teach (and fail to teach) rural children—work widely
acclaimed for its lyrical prose and eloquence. A respected and
inspiring educator, Paul's writer-in-residence involvements
included St. Olaf and Concordia Colleges, The University of
Minnesota, The Superior Studies Program, as well as lectures and
workshops in public schools, churches, bookstores, government
and environmental organizations. He won both the Minnesota
Book and Lifetime Achievement Awards, served on the board of
the National Endowment for the Humanities, and in the 1980s
edited *The Worthington Globe*—an award-winning newspaper.
His unpublished work includes several natural history
manuscripts, a personal journey, numerous lectures, poetry, fiction
and a compelling memoir exploring his struggle with depression
and the mental health treatment system. Paul took his own life
in Duluth, Minnesota, on February 22, 2004, at the age of 56.

Table of Contents—

Remembering Paul

Thomas K. Dean,
Editor

The Grace of Grass & Water

I first met Paul Gruchow where I should have: in a book. The only better place would have been meeting up with him walking on the prairie or through the woods. The essay was "Winter," from Paul's first book, *Journal of a Prairie Year*. In language eloquent, simple, deep, and profound, he describes a prairie walk on a winter day, turning starkness and simplicity into great beauty—beauty in word, image, and truth. I knew Paul Gruchow was a writer I needed to know better when I read these lines: "If I could explain the sound of a footstep upon the snow or come to know the underlying principles that govern the meandering of the snow along a fenceline, I should then be attuned in a new way to the largely unheard and mysterious music of the universe"(5).

In his self-effacing way, Paul claims that "I am unequipped as the next person. I listen in the dead of winter to the song the snow sings, and strain as I might, I cannot make it out"(5). But Paul is too modest here. If anyone were equipped to hear the song of the snow, or even the music of the universe, it was Paul. And he did. And he reported, described, inscribed, essayed, and sang that music in writings that must stand as among not only the best writing from the Midwest, but the best writing about nature and place anywhere.

Of the "music of the universe," Paul was willing to admit that "the mystery has captivated me, and under the spell of it, I have meandered, like the drifts of snow, across the wide prairies"(5). For fifteen years now, I have meandered, figuratively speaking, with Paul across the wide prairies, captivated by their mystery, seeking the song of snows, grasses, and woods. Paul Gruchow was the one who first articulated for me the beauty and meaning of the prairie, of the gorgeous bleakness of winter, of love for the Midwest, of the

3

profundity of nature. Very few people understand the necessary
and intimate connections between humanity and environment,
between geography and society, between community and nature,
better than Paul Gruchow. Paul's writings were, have been, and
will continue to be the guiding lights for me as I have worked to
articulate my own ideas about place.

I first met Paul in person one November in the early 1990s
at Southwest State University's Marshall Festival, a week-long
celebration of Midwestern rural writing. Southwestern Minnesota,
where the gently rolling river valleys of eastern Minnesota
give way to the imposing flatness of the Great Plains' edge, is
a beautiful but forbidding land, especially in late fall. Despite
our own Midwestern roots, my wife and I were awestruck by
the far horizon, the lone farmhouses with their single barnyard
lights shining lonely beacons at night, the rarity of trees. At the
conference, Door County, Wisconsin writer Norbert Blei opined
that, arriving in Marshall the previous evening, he thought he
had been dropped onto the moon. But this was the homeland
of Paul Gruchow, who grew up in southwestern Minnesota and
made much of his early career there, as editor and co-owner of
the *Worthington Globe*. Although I have since lived on the western
Minnesota prairie, I have realized the gentler eastern prairie is my
spiritual home, and that is why I am here. But it is Paul Gruchow's
prairie landscape, and his profound sermons on its beauties and
depths, that remain my inspiration for what it means to live in the
tall grasses of the middle land.

Paul was a reader at the Marshall Festival. I was not prepared
for the intensity of the experience. Behind a lone podium at the
head of a large public university institutional auditorium of sterile

1970s vintage, an unremarkable, rather rumpled man stood. Not very tall, balding, with a scraggly short beard and round glasses that obscured eyes I was sure must have had supernatural powers that penetrated to the depths of nature, Paul Gruchow announced in a slightly gravelly voice that he was going to read from a new book he was working on. For the next half hour, I and my fellow audience members sat transfixed. In a voice no one would call mellifluous, Paul read an essay nevertheless with a lyricism, a depth of feeling, an intensity that remains unmatched in my experience. I have been brought nearly to tears only once at a reading, and it was that day in Marshall, Minnesota, listening to Paul Gruchow read an essay about the birth of his daughter as his own mother lay dying, the bleak January trip fighting time and Minnesota winter to let grandmother and granddaughter meet at least once in a hospital room in Montevideo, Minnesota, and the phone call when the Gruchow family arrived back home in St. Paul informing them that Mother had passed away. More than a recounting of a highly emotional experience, this essay, which now begins *Grass Roots*, was a profound meditation on the relationship between place and time.

I met Paul personally for the first time only briefly a couple of days later. I had arrived too late to find a seat for a reading by Bill Holm and Howard Mohr. Huddled with a group of people in the back corner near the coat racks, I found myself standing next to Paul Gruchow. I briefly introduced myself, expressed my deep admiration for his writing and his reading at the Festival. With shy grace, Paul politely thanked me.

Several years later, teaching at Michigan State University, I was rapidly developing a deep interest in the idea of place. I was growing to see the interconnections between natural, built, social, and cultural environments, the warp and weave of human existence that resolved itself into, fundamentally, one's grounding in a particular place. And underlying all of this thinking, and this feeling, were the work and the words of Paul Gruchow.

I decided to call my inspiration. I am not one to call people I do not know brazenly out of the blue. But as the Northfield, Minnesota phone rang a few times, I kept telling myself that I was doing this because I knew Paul must be a kind and generous man. I knew (well, hoped) that if he told me to get lost, he would do so politely. Soon I heard a voice say, simply, "Paul Gruchow." I briefly introduced myself, said we had met fleetingly a few years before though I was sure he did not remember me, and launched into my idea for an organization, based in academia but reaching out to the public, that would work to develop understandings of place and devotions to community. I wondered if he would serve on an advisory board for such an enterprise, and if he would be able to appear as the keynote speaker at a small conference I was organizing on the Michigan State campus that next spring.

No one was around to pick me up off the floor when he said, "Sure." But that was Paul. He didn't suffer fools gladly, or at all. He could be merciless in his excoriation of phonies and dunderheads. But he was generous, perhaps to a fault, to people and to causes that he believed in. To this day I thank my good fortune that I was of the latter category rather than the former. In our phone conversation, Paul talked a bit about how important it was for people to understand and practice the kinds of attitudes and feelings toward place that I was describing. Ironically, he was the one who, more than anyone, had helped me find the words and

the voice to articulate the very ideas which I was now sharing with
him.

On the night of the Gruchows' arrival in East Lansing for
the conference, my wife Susan and I trucked our two small
children, Paul, and his wife Nancy out to the Travelers Club
International Restaurant and Tuba Museum in nearby Okemos.
The pretentious part of the name is both an accurate description
and a joke. Housed in an old hardware store, with skrutchy
wooden tables and chairs and a lunch counter crowded together
in a homey atmosphere, the TCIRTM serves funky international
cuisine and downhome Midwestern diner fare. If you want
African Mujadarrah, you can get it there. If you want a grilled
cheese sandwich, you can get it there. And while waiting for your
food, you can admire and compare the mixed conglomeration
of dinnerware placed at your table or—really—the world-class
collection of tubas ringing the walls. It was a perfect place to bring
the Gruchows.

We were lucky that it was a Friday night. To our delight, there
was also music, a crackerjack folk and bluegrass ensemble. The
Gruchows passed our one-year-old daughter Sylvia back and
forth between them, setting her on their laps and bouncing their
knees to the music, laughing at the bubbles coming from our
baby's mouth. Nancy sensed four-year-old Nathaniel's occasional
impatience and fished in her purse, pulling out a small purple
calculator to keep his small fingers occupied. When Nathaniel
was reluctant to give it up at the end of the evening, Nancy
laughed and said he could keep it. We still have "Mrs. Gruchow's
Calculator" to this day. It was a memorable evening—simple,
fun, and warm. The music, laughter, and kindness were perfectly

complemented by the closeness of the strange and wonderful yet folksy tuba museum. It was like we had known the Gruchows for our entire lives.

As the two days of their visit ensued, I gained my first insights into the foibles and troubles of Paul Gruchow. During the next night's dinner, before his public reading, the mood was much quieter than the previous evening. Paul ate very little, perhaps nothing at all. When he visited the rest room, Nancy apologized for Paul's mood and his lack of appetite. She said he always got really nervous before readings. I almost couldn't believe my ears. The best public reader I had ever heard, and he got nervous? The quiet power of his oratory, the controlled intensity actually masking terror? Paul was a transformed man when he took the podium later that evening, mesmerizing as he took us deeply into his beautiful language and his profound thought. And underneath he was quaking in his boots?

By an amazing coincidence, I was to begin a teaching job at Moorhead State University (now Minnesota State University Moorhead) the following year, and, by gosh, Paul Gruchow would be there with me on the prairie. He was returning to a visiting teaching position at Concordia College in Moorhead as well. I count as one of my life's good fortunes my personal friendship with Paul Gruchow, developed over those ensuing years in Moorhead. To this day, I warmly conjure several tableaux.

I still envision Paul simply walking by our dining room window on his way to campus, smiling broadly and waving vigorously as he quickly pumped his short legs like pistons. One bright morning, my visiting father-in-law looked out the window and said, "Hey, there's a professor!" Sure enough, it was Paul—bearded, rumpled, bespectacled, carrying a book—power-walking past our dining room window. I laughed. "That's Paul Gruchow!" I said, and waved. Seeing the joy and verve on Paul's face in these moments, his body no doubt invigorated by the crisp northern prairie air, I found it difficult to imagine him in the depths of psychological misery, which, I soon came to understand, he often experienced.

I still conjure our coffee dates in Moorhead. They were rarely, if ever, profound. Rather than the deep meanings of "literature" or "nature," we would talk about frustrations over institutional politics, the shockingly poor skills or soaring talents of our students, the possibilities and hopes for both of our futures, the foibles of life in Fargo/Moorhead, our families. It was during one of these coffee dates that Paul revealed to me that he had never applied for a job. In his half-century of life, someone or other had always managed to come to him with work. As I grew to know him better, I realized that's how he conducted his life—a shy, insecure man at the core, letting people and opportunities come to him and his greatness (though he would never have acknowledged the latter). Yet Paul lived a life of anxiety, of constant worry that the world would discover him a fraud and stop coming to him.

Nevertheless, Paul also remained fearless about his participation in that world. Paul both admired and scoffed at, respectively, the knowledge and the pomposity of academia. He laughed at the world of colleges and universities with satirical abandon, but he also laughed at his own self-perceived inadequacies and stumblings within it. He got the last laugh, though. My favorite academic story that Paul told was about how he flummoxed the human resources office at Concordia. Well into his visiting professorship, a kind woman called Paul one day and said, "Dr. Gruchow [which Paul found amusing], I'm afraid we don't have a copy of your certified transcript showing your degree in your file."

Paul replied, "I'm sorry, but I don't have a degree."

The woman, unphased, said, "Well, that's ok if you don't have a doctorate. Many of our visiting professors don't."

Paul said, no doubt quite matter-of-factly, "No, you don't understand. I don't have a degree of any kind. I never graduated from college."

Only silence answered him on the other end of the line. Eventually, the woman simply said, "Well, let me get back to you." She never did. And Paul continued to teach at Concordia for several more semesters.

I will also always hold dear our walks through the streets of Moorhead. One Halloween, I had dressed up all day at school as Walt Whitman, replete with a big wool overcoat from the Moorhead Goodwill under which I had stuffed a pillow, a cheap fake gray beard, and a straw hat. Late that afternoon, walking through the elm-bowered streets of Moorhead over to the Concordia campus, getting a little hot in my outfit in the breezy, dusty, and dusky yet surprisingly warm late fall air, I arrived at Concordia's Academy Hall and made my way upstairs to Paul's office. He was sitting hunched over his metal desk, grading papers, his disheveled office littered with papers and books. I just barged into his doorway and boomed, "Unscrew the locks from the doors!/Unscrew the doors themselves from their jambs!/Whoever degrades another degrades me,/And whatever is done or said returns at last to me!" Paul just looked up with a big grin and a hearty guffaw. On our way to the coffee shop, Paul flinched not a whit at walking down the street with a guy in a Whitman costume as if it were the most natural thing in the world.

One unseasonably warm spring, as we walked home together on a gorgeous night following an event I had organized at which he spoke, warm breezes up from Missouri and Iowa rather than down from Alberta and Saskatchewan wafted over us in the dim glow of streetlights. Flowers and trees were not blooming yet, but temperatures in the 40s or 50s in the darkness of evening were a joy after winter in the Red River Valley. Paul said, rather simply, "Boy, this weather is beautiful."

I nodded and looked around, following up with, "Yeah, but I bet the other shoe is gonna drop before we know it. We can't be done with snow and cold yet."

Paul chuckled and looked at me. "Boy, you *are* fitting in up here, aren't you?"

I laughed, too, of course, but I welcomed Paul's needling about my dark pessimism. If it meant I was becoming Minnesotan, if it meant I was sending out taproots into home, that was a good thing.

In those simple moments, we truly shared a community, a neighborhood, the Red River Valley of the North, and the mutual work of teaching good reading and writing. But I also came to know the darkness and sadness of Paul's depression during those years, difficulties so deep that he was hospitalized when the pressures of teaching and of life in general overwhelmed him. Still, as I and my family moved back to Iowa and as Paul moved to northeastern Minnesota, I was fortunate to see him in all his robustness another time or two.

My other landscape of the heart is the Minnesota North Woods, and one year we arranged to stop and visit the Gruchows on our way home from the Boundary Waters area. Paul and Nancy had bought a beautiful, sprawling home on an acreage outside of Two Harbors. We pulled into the long gravel driveway, and three large black dogs bounded out to greet us. And there came Paul, out the front door, smiling broadly as usual, waving vigorously at us. He looked good, even succumbing to fashion, in a way, with a new buzz cut. We admired the addition he and Nancy were building on the house, a long and open space with large windows looking out onto a pine-scattered meadow. Paul was going to put his library here, do his writing here. The baby grand piano was already in place even as construction ensued around it.

We talked, laughed, and drank a lot of coffee. Our kids, when they got tired of sitting on our laps, lounged on the hammock on the back screened-in porch and laughed as they let the dogs in and out. We railed against the state of the country under a regressive and oppressive new administration in Washington, D.C., excoriating the Undersecretary of Agriculture for Rural Development whom George W. Bush wanted to appoint, and who, to my embarrassment, hailed from Iowa. With whom else would a discussion about the Undersecretary of Agriculture for Rural Development even take place, let alone take place with proper gusto and melodrama, than with Paul Gruchow?

Interestingly, the man who had never applied for a job in his life had now done so, and had gotten it. Paul was traveling the 20 miles or so to Duluth several days a week to an institution where he would talk through the horrors and delusions and pain of, literally, schizophrenic murderers. Paul told us of how they reported what they saw to him—devils standing on the other side of doorways, the men paralyzed with fear, even though they often knew intellectually that nothing stood before them. Paul talked about his work with a zeal and zest I had rarely seen in him. He was even thinking about going back to school to enroll in a mental health nursing program at the University of Minnesota-Duluth. Paul seemed to have found a purpose that in that moment rivaled his love of nature and place, which he had been writing about for decades.

Within the next year, though, Paul's life spiraled downward. His marriage fell apart. His new career plans in mental health nursing did not work out. More hospitalizations. He was still living, but now alone, in the house in Two Harbors. We stopped by to visit him again on our way home from our North Woods summer retreat the next year. We told Paul of a wonderful new remote cabin we had found to stay in the following year, on a small pond two or three miles down a primitive logging road. I could see the image's wonders seeping into Paul's mind, approbation spreading across his face as a smile. One of my most meaningful moments with Paul occurred then. He told me and Susan that we were doing something very special for our kids, creating a place for them beyond home that would remain special throughout their lives. Just as "digging in" at home is necessary for dwelling in place, so too is frequent return to a meaningful other place. For us it was the Minnesota North Woods. Paul said for him and his native Minnesotan children, it was Mexico. No matter how much other travel one did, how many far-flung corners of the world one might explore, a regular return to a special family place is an anchor in life, one that many contemporary Americans neglect to establish. I never sought Paul's approval, although I welcomed it. But more important to me was his wisdom, when he shared it. I even imagined Paul visiting us for a few days in the large cabin the next year. He seemed quite taken with our description of the place, and I was desperately casting about for small ways to salve his loneliness.

As we parted ways, the atmosphere was decidedly more muted than the previous year. We told Paul once again that we were sorry for the breakup of his marriage, that we hoped he would remain well, and that if somehow we could offer him any help, we would. He always was welcome to Iowa City, and we always had a bed for him. We made our farewells and pulled out of the long gravel driveway. I looked back at Paul standing alone near his house, waving. We waved back from afar. That was the last time I ever saw Paul Gruchow.

After that, communication with Paul became much more difficult and sporadic. I unsuccessfully tried to get him to Iowa City for a reading or talk at least a couple of times. I did manage to contact him once more in what would be his last summer. I received an e-mail from him, a short message full of desperation. He had quit writing and speaking entirely. He told me he had no wife, no home, no job, no health insurance. He had health problems even beyond his depression. No one was looking to hire a man in his mid-50s who had been institutionalized multiple times. I immediately replied, though not sure exactly what to say. I said that I would keep my eye out for some kind of employment for him in Iowa City, a community I knew he would love. I would ask my friends if they knew of any positions for him. I would do anything I possibly could for him; all he had to do was ask. And

I said I was very concerned about him, and I hoped he knew that a lot of people cared about him. I never received Paul's promised message back.

In late February 2004, Paul Gruchow took his own life. He had attempted suicide at least four previous times since 2001. Although not entirely unexpected, his loss was, and remains, a profound shock to me. Paul was a man so full of life, so full of talent, so full of the world, so full of possibilities, so full of beautiful words and thoughts. But he was also a man full of darkness and desperation, and full of torments I will never fully understand.

I wish Paul could have stopped his suffering, and could have done so in a less tragic way. I wish something—medicine, soul work, love, anything—could have made him better and done so while keeping his humanity intact. Like so many others, I wish I could have helped him through his troubles. Many, many people's love for him, and for his work, was not enough to hold him up, to hold him together, to hold him with us. At the time of his death, Paul had finished a new book manuscript detailing his mental disease from the inside. Paul had said it was frank and funny, but those who have read it say it is also harrowing. I leave it to others who knew him better to decide whether or not the manuscript should be published. On the one hand, we should know and understand his suffering, his life, as much as possible. At the same time, while we honor, respect, and strive to understand Paul in his entirety, I want to remember him mostly as the artist and sage of the prairie and woods that he was.

Yet, no doubt, the two sides of Paul Gruchow—the sage of nature and the tortured soul—are inseparable. It may very well be that Paul was the artist and visionary that he was because of, at least in part, his mental disease. The cliché goes that great artists are nearly always tortured. I have never fully believed that, at least as a universal principle, but I have come to realize that this was almost certainly the case with Paul Gruchow. My attraction to Paul's work has always been the intensity and depth he brings to his language, to his penetrating observations about nature, community, and place, about the human experience. The brightness of the light of his gifts was no doubt supported in many ways by the darkness of their terrors. I still marvel at the near-aching passion he could bring to a meditation on prairie grass, the universe-spanning concentration of power with which he could infuse a recollection of a North Woods thunderstorm. That Paul had to suffer demonic torment in his mind and soul in order to bring such exquisite splendor to us breaks my heart.

One of my favorite passages by Paul begins *Grass Roots: The Universe of Home*, which I consider his finest book: "What if one's life were not a commodity, not something to be bartered to the highest bidder, or made to order? What if one's life were governed by needs more fundamental than acceptance or admiration? What if one were simply to stay home and plant some manner of garden?"(3). I think of that passage often when we work in our gardens at home. A few years ago, we planted native prairie grasses and flowers in a circle of mud in our backyard. Our prairie patch is hardly a contribution to restoring the native ecosystem, yet it is more than decorative landscaping. It is a declaration of place, an honoring of where we are, a reminder of what has been lost in our Midwest, and a lesson for our children about the capabilities for beauty that nature owns in the middle land. Here, especially, in this small patch, as I tend the grasses and flowers, Paul's words, spirit, and kindness revisit me. I remember his important lesson of home-as-garden as the little bluestem, side oats gramma, Indian grass, prairie violets, asters, blazing stars, and spiderwort grow and bloom. Maybe, wherever he is now, Paul has found the music of the universe he said he could not hear. Maybe he is now singing that music in harmony, at last, with an existence he found overwhelmingly gorgeous yet, in his mortality, brutally unbearable. I hope that a few grace notes from Paul's song find their way into our backyard prairie patch.

I will always grieve for the loss of Paul Gruchow, and I will always remain saddened by the tragedy of his life. I will also be saddened by opportunities lost: ironically, nearly all of my interactions with Paul were indoors; our "someday" walks on the prairie or woods were never realized. But I intend for my larger memory of him to remain more positive. His work inspired my own, and that won't change. If I can, in my own small ways, keep Paul's spirit of love for nature, place, community, the prairie, the woods, and the middle land alive through my own stumbling work, I will be happy. I will remember and revisit and enjoy his essays until I die myself one day. As I continue to plumb the mysteries of the North Woods with my family, I will keep Paul's grace of the wild with me. As I continue to live a good life on the Iowa prairie, I will tap Paul's spirit through the deep grass roots and honor the universe of home. I miss you, Paul. And you will always remain my inspiration and friend.

This book is one of those small ways in which I hope to keep Paul's spirit and work alive. Steve Semken and I asked a number of Paul's friends and colleagues to contribute to this volume in ways

The Grace of Grass & Water

that would not only honor his memory, but even more importantly advance his vision and his work. Not only are we able to present to you one of Paul's last writings—an essay originally published in the Ice Cube Press's Harvest Book *Prairie Roots: Call of the Wild*— but also a collection of essays that range across analysis of Paul's writing, environmental writing inspired by his good example, reminiscences of meaningful moments with Paul, and meditations on his influence, past, present, and future.

This volume was something I wanted to see happen since shortly after Paul left us. I knew an appropriate amount of time needed to pass, and I think we have, at this point, assimilated the tragedy of his passing respectfully and significantly. I thank Steve Semken for being willing to publish this tribute to Paul and this advancement of his work, and for his tremendous help in gathering a remarkable constellation of writers. I thank Lou Martinelli, Paul's literary executor and a contributor to this volume, for his support, good advice, and dedication to perpetuating the life and work of Paul Gruchow. I thank the contributors to this volume, wonderful writers and dear friends of Paul. Their willingness to share, their talents, and their devotion to the man and vision we honor here are inspiring. I also thank all the other writers and friends whom we contacted about this volume who universally offered their support, but for various—and good—reasons were unable to contribute their writing. I pass along my best wishes to the Gruchow family, who I hope are able to take some comfort, through this volume, in knowing that many people loved and were inspired by Paul, at the same time we understand the difficulties that his life created.

I thank you, our readers, for participating in this project by reading our work, for thinking about and remembering Paul, and for, I hope, bringing his vision forward into a world that is both distressed and beautiful. Paul would want us to see and feel both of those aspects, and in so doing, and then acting upon that understanding, make the world a better place. I hope this book helps you do that in at least some small way.

But most of all, I thank Paul for being with us, if for a shorter time than we would have hoped, for being who he was, for sharing his great talent with the world, even when it hurt, and hurt deeply. I hope he knows that, thanks to him, many, many people know the world's awesomeness, beauty, mystery, and profundity in marvelous and transformative ways, that the grace of grass and water will always be with us.

—Iowa City, Iowa, March, 2007

Works Cited

Gruchow, Paul. *Grass Roots: The Universe of Home*. Minneapolis: Milkweed Editions, 1995.

—. *Journal of a Prairie Year*. Minneapolis: University of Minnesota Press, 1985.

Thomas Dean is Special Assistant to the President for communications and research at The University of Iowa, from which he earned a Ph.D. in English. He founded and directs the Iowa Project on Place Studies and is adjunct assistant professor of Literature, Science, and the Arts. A Pushcart Prize nominee, Dean has published in *Little Village*, *The Wapsipinicon Almanac*, *here: the magazine of where we are*, *The Iowa Source*, and several book anthologies from the Ice Cube Press. His first book of essays, *Under A Midland Sky*, is forthcoming from the Ice Cube Press.

The Meaning
of Natural History

Paul Gruchow

Henry David Thoreau, who just barely qualified for admission, got his formal training at Harvard College. The system of education at Harvard in 1833 emphasized rote memorization and good behavior. Classroom discussion was out of the question, and even lectures by professors were discouraged. The model student was passive, dutiful, worshipped the ancients, and doubted the advisability of anything contemporary—roughly the reverse of contemporary intellectual fashion. You could be punished academically for skipping chapel, wearing a coat of a color other than black (although Thoreau, too poor to afford a new coat, was tolerated for his old green one), and making inappropriate noises in the dining hall. Of the 63 members of Thoreau's class, 44 eventually found themselves subject to disciplinary action by the faculty. Students, not surprisingly, hated the place. During Thoreau's years at Harvard, the system provoked both a petition campaign, which Thoreau supported—students said the place promoted superficial scholarship—and a riot, from which he was absent, and which was suppressed with rigor a banana republic dictator might have admired. The leaders of the revolt were prosecuted in public court, and the entire sophomore class, with three exceptions, were expelled. The curriculum, designed mainly to turn out ministers, emphasized the study of classical languages, mathematics, and philosophy. Modern languages, although not yet academically respectable in the 1830s, were offered as electives. In addition to the mandatory Greek and Latin, in which he became fluent, Thoreau studied Italian, French, German, and Spanish. The English instruction was not in literature—post-Roman writing was not respectable then either—but in rhetoric. Thoreau had only one class in modern literature—on German and Scandinavian writing, taught by Henry Wadsworth Longfellow—and a single class in biology, a natural history term taught by the college librarian, for whom the subject was an avocation. Both were ventures beyond the required curriculum. Thoreau was, by the standards of his time, a competent student, graduating in the upper third of his class. His teachers thought him an able, if not outstanding, scholar. He might have become a good entomologist if Emerson hadn't spoiled him, his natural history teacher said. His Greek professor, Cornelius Conway Felton, later president of Harvard, remembered him as a scholar of talent, but of such pertinacious oddity in literary matters that his writing will probably never do him any justice. The most promising writer in Thoreau's class, his English professor judged, was one Horace Morison, whose sole work, *Pebbles from the Seashore*, you surely must know. Harvard did offer, despite its deficiencies as an educational institution, a splendid library of 50,000 volumes, which Thoreau patronized for the rest of his days. There he began his lifelong habit of far-flung and systematic reading. During his college years he read his way through the 21-volume Chalmers anthology, *The English Poets*. He studied the Greek poets, read Shakespeare and Homer, devoured travel books, and sampled the works of such contemporary American writers as Cooper, Irving, and Longfellow. Later, his reading would expand to include works of science and natural history, of religion and philosophy, and such accounts of native American life and culture as were then available. He read not only in English, but also in the six languages he had learned at college, and, more haltingly, in Sanskrit and Hebrew. Thoreau not only read voraciously, but he began in college to keep the extensive notebooks—a million words of which still survive—on which he drew when he settled into his life's work. He also began, in college, the practice of slipping away into the nearby woods and fields to see what was up in nature. One winter while he was at Harvard, he made daily visits to the nest of a weasel in the hollow of an old apple tree. When his neighbor and mentor, Ralph Waldo Emerson, suggested to the young graduate that he make his journal systematic—the date was October 22, 1837—the tools of Thoreau's intellectual life were complete. From then on, with remarkable steadfastness of purpose, he practiced a threefold discipline: mornings for writing, afternoons for walking, evening for reading and reflection. Over the next twenty-some years, he wrote an immortal book; started, with his brother, an elementary school that was a hundred years ahead of its time; designed the best pencil then available; made still-reliable surveys of the countryside around Concord, Massachusetts; kept a three-million-word journal that is in itself one of the monuments of American culture; and, we have only recently learned, left behind at his premature death the first serious work of ecology, although the scientific idea of ecology had not yet been invented.

John Muir, born in Scotland, was raised at hard labor on the Wisconsin frontier by a father who was tyrannical, anti-intellectual, and a religious extremist. Forbidden to read in the evenings, Muir found an outlet for his lively intelligence in invention. He experimented with waterwheels and windmills and then with a series of remarkable clocks, all of the pieces whittled from hickory, which he assembled with the aid only of a book that taught him the laws of the pendulum. He was forbidden to take apart the family clock to see firsthand how these devices were conventionally made. The first of his clocks was shaped like

The Grace of Grass & Water

a sawmill and not only kept time but registered dates, lit fires and a lamp, and could be set to upend a bed at any hour. Muir called it his early rising machine. He made a clock shaped like a scythe, in which each individual part also had the shape of a scythe or of an arrow: it kept accurate time for more than fifty years. And he made a clock meant to be hung from the barn and designed to be read from the adjacent fields: its main hand was fourteen feet long; but his father, fearing that it would attract crowds, refused to let him install it. Muir also made thermometers, pyrometers, hygrometers and a barometer as a youth. Among these was a thermometer built on the same scale as the barn clock, mounted high on the Muir house, and so sensitive that it registered the body heat of a person approaching to within four or five feet of it. An equally sensitive thermometer, fashioned from an old washboard, and two of his early rising machines became Muir's ticket to freedom. He demonstrated these devices at the Temple of Art at the Wisconsin State Fair in 1860. They caused a public sensation, won a prize, and landed him a job with another inventor who was exhibiting a steam-powered ice boat at the fair. Muir was to tend the boat in exchange for lessons in mechanical drawing, which he never got. Trial runs that winter at Prairie du Chien, Wisconsin, on the Mississippi, proved the boat a flop, and Muir soon departed for the University of Wisconsin in Madison, "desperately hungry and thirsty for knowledge," he said, "and willing to endure anything to get it." He was admitted there, despite his paucity of formal education, as a first year student, enrolled in chemistry, geology, Latin, and Greek, the science courses for himself, the language courses for his mother, who hoped he would become a preacher. He was conspicuous on campus for his homespun dress and his unshorn and unkempt hair and beard, but he was also soon marked as the best chemistry student at the university and became locally celebrated for his inventions. These included a new early rising machine, a bed triggered by sunlight to dump its occupant onto the floor; a loafer's chair rigged so that sitting in it fired off a pistol loaded with a blank cartridge; and a study desk run by a clock that dropped a book onto a shelf, gave the user a predetermined number of minutes to examine it, and then swept it aside to be replaced with another. Students showing parents and dignitaries the campus sights invariably took them around to see Muir and his inventions. But he had no money, and the Civil War, which Muir spent in Canada, intervened. In the end, he completed only two and a half years of work at the university. After he left Madison, Muir wandered and botanized along the Canadian shores of the Great Lakes, and did factory work, inventing, on speculation in the finished products, machines that doubled the standard rate of production of hardwood broom handles and rake teeth. Before the 30,000 broom handles and 6,000 rakes he had made could be sold, the factory burned, destroying not only his inventory but also his notebooks and herbaria. In 1866, with just enough money for his train fare, he returned to the United States, getting as far as Indianapolis, where he found work in a factory making carriage parts. His extraordinary abilities as a technical manager were soon noticed, and Muir was given wide latitude to make improvements. He invented machinery to make complete wheels, except for the iron tires, without hand labor. He improved the efficiency of the system of belts that operated the equipment, did time and motion studies—these were among the first such studies ever done—leading to improvements in the organization of the plant, and recommended shorter work days for laborers. Ten-hour days were then standard, and were still regarded as an extremely liberal concession to labor, but Muir showed that the precipitous drop in efficiency after the first eight hours made longer days counterproductive. But Muir disregarded his own advice. One day in March of 1867, while working alone late at night on a new belt in the factory, he lost his grip on the file he was using and it flew up and pierced his right eye, which went blind. He recuperated for a month. Eventually the sight returned to his eye, but his factory days, which had brought him up against what he called "the gobble gobble school of economics," were over. When he had sufficiently recovered from his accident, he set out on foot, walked a thousand miles to Miami, caught a boat to Cuba (where his plan to continue on to South America was foiled by a bout with malaria), went to California instead (by way of Panama), got off his ship in San Francisco, walked straight through the town and into the Sierra Nevada Mountains, and never looked back. Muir wandered the Sierras alone for months at a stretch, eager to experience everything they had to offer, to the extent of riding out a thunderstorm in the top of a tall spruce tree, just to see what that would be like. He learned, he said, that even trees do a good bit of traveling. He figured out the role of glaciation in shaping the Sierras, his work proving more accurate than that of the leading American scientist of the day, Louis Aggasiz, who was also wrong, unlike Muir, about Darwin. He wrote several enduring volumes of natural history, campaigned for the formation of the national park system, founded the Sierra Club, and prospered as one of the first big fruit growers in California's Central Valley.

Rachel Carson grew up in the countryside near Pittsburgh, Pennsylvania. She was a sickly child who frequently missed school and perhaps on that account was something of a loner. She found companionship in the woods and fields surrounding her home. She was also precocious, sailing through her schooling, which included a degree in biology, magna cum laude, from the Pennsylvania College for Women; a postgraduate internship at the Marine Biological Laboratory at Woods Hole, where she saw the ocean for the first time; and a Master's degree in zoology, with a concentration in genetics, from Johns Hopkins University. Carson, knowing from an early age that she wanted to be a writer, enrolled, when she entered the Philadelphia College for Women, as an English major. In her junior year she took the introductory biology courses to fulfill a distribution requirement, expecting to find the experience distasteful. But she loved the classes so much that, to the dismay of her English Department mentor, for whom she was the star student, she switched her major at the last minute, and over the next several years gave little further thought to writing. One would not have been encouraged to believe in an English Department in the 1920s that science could be a suitable subject for literature. Indeed, although a strong case can be made that the two distinctive contributions of American writers to literature are the short story and the natural history essay, it is still true that Literature, when it is thought of with a capital L, means poems, novels, and plays. The essay is still treated as the literary equivalent of an etude in music, a minor form, suitable for use in instructing the young, but not in itself of any serious artistic or intellectual interest. Carson emerged from college in the first years of the Great Depression when employment of any kind was hard to find, much less for a woman scientist. She had the good luck, however, to interview with Elmer Higgens of the U.S. Bureau of Fisheries, a distinguished biologist but no writer, who had just been assigned the task of writing a series of radio scripts about the Bureau's work. When he learned that Carson could write, Higgens took a gamble and hired her. The radio series proved so successful that Higgens edited the scripts into a government booklet, asking Carson for an introduction. He rejected the text she produced, telling her it was too good for a government pamphlet and urging her to send it instead to the *Atlantic Monthly*. Carson, who knew that the magazine had also published Thoreau and Muir, did not have as much confidence in her work as her employer. She filed the piece away in a desk drawer. In the meantime, her father and older sister died, and Carson took on the task of supporting her family, augmenting her income at the Bureau with part-time teaching at the University of Maryland. When a position opened as a junior aquatic biologist in the Bureau, she took the Civil Service test, earned the highest score, and was hired and assigned as assistant editor in the Information Section. Her radio scripts had by then attracted the attention of the Sunday editor of the *Baltimore Sun*, who signed her on as an occasional contributor. Her success there finally gave her the courage to send the introduction she had tucked away to the *Atlantic Monthly*. The magazine bought it, the piece led to a contract with Simon and Schuster, and that resulted, in November, 1941, in the publication of *Under the Sea Wind*, regarded by some critics as her best book. It got lost, however, in the national trauma of the opening days of World War II, attracted little notice, and sold poorly. The Bureau of Fisheries became the U.S. Fish and Wildlife Service. Carson rose steadily through its ranks, becoming, by 1947, editor in chief of the Information Division. Her wartime duties included writing a series of pamphlets on the cooking of various seafoods, which the government was promoting as an alternative to the increasingly scarce supply of red meats. This assignment amused her co-workers, who knew that she abhorred all housework, and especially loathed cooking. During the 1940s, as Carson worked by day at the Fish and Wildlife Service, she also moonlighted as a freelancer for several national magazines, nurturing the ambition to write another book. The idea she settled on, and got a contract for from Oxford University Press, was to write a biography of the sea. She had looked for such a book, she said, and had not been able to find it, as, of course, she couldn't: the idea was as radically original as Thoreau's *Walden*. With *The Sea Around Us*, as the book came eventually to be called, Carson was inventing an entirely new kind of nature writing. She labored at the book through the late 1940s, writing at home far into the night after she had come home from her day job. She was a slow and meticulous writer, a perfectionist not only about her style but also about her facts. The book synthesized information gathered from hundreds of dense texts and obscure scientific articles, and from correspondence with marine biologists and oceanographers around the world. It was to be an unusual book not only in its biographical form but also in that it was primarily based not on firsthand observation but on library work, although she did supplement it with as much field investigation as she could find the time for, learning, among other things in the course of her preparations, to scuba dive. Carson was to the literature of natural history what her contemporary I.F. Stone was to political journalism, a writer whose

The Grace of Grass & Water

authority derived not from being an eyewitness—a notably unreliable kind of testimony, in any case—but on having read all the fine print that everybody else skipped. Even before *The Sea Around Us* was published in 1951, it attracted significant attention, earning her a fellowship for promising young writers and a $1,000 prize, for an excerpt published in the *Yale Review*, for the best science writing of 1950. But Carson's big break came in the spring of 1951, when the *New Yorker* published three long and celebrated excerpts from the book under the title *Profiles from the Sea*. When the book was finally launched in July of 1951, it landed straight on the best-seller lists, and stayed there for the next 83 weeks. What is more, Oxford University Press reissued *Under the Sea Wind* the next year, and it, too, became a best-seller, making Carson one of those rare writers to have two simultaneous best-sellers, a feat normally reserved for the John Grishams and Danielle Steeles of the world. From then on, she was showered with invitations to speak and publish, with prizes and honorary degrees. Carson at first shied away from doing the book that altered contemporary history. With her literary success, she had been able to quit her job and to buy a house in Maine on the shore of the ocean she loved so much. After a third book on the subject, *The Edge of the Sea*, which started as a conventional guidebook and evolved into an account of three shoreline ecosystems, one of the first books of this kind, Carson felt she had done what she could with the sea as a subject. She considered writing a book about evolution and decided against it. While she was still mulling the possibilities for a new subject, one of her friends sent her a copy of a letter she had sent to the *Boston Globe* protesting the aerial spraying of Cape Cod with DDT to control mosquitoes. Carson looked into the practice, was disturbed by what she learned, and wrote a magazine piece on the dangers of overusing DDT, but editors found it unconvincing—it was scientifically unorthodox—and nobody was willing to take the piece. Then, in 1957, the government announced plans to spray Long Island with DDT to control gypsy moths. Carson, who knew that gypsy moths are forest creatures and that Long Island is not forested, found this idea absurd. A group of Long Islanders sued to prevent the spraying. Carson wrote to E. B. White, suggesting that he cover the trial. White replied that she ought to do it herself, so she made plans to write about the trial for the *New Yorker* and to collect the pieces in a small volume. She set out, as she had done with the sea, to master her subject, reading everything she could find, ferreting through journals in medicine, organic chemistry, agronomy, and other disciplines, and initiating correspondence with scientists all over the world who might shed some light on the matter. Before long, what had been meant to be a brief collection of essays blossomed into a full-scale examination of the ecological implications of pesticides. Carson was not the first person to address this issue. There had been other books, but they had been either eloquent books written by authors with a shaky grasp of science, or books of sound scientific analysis written by authors with no literary ability. Carson brought a unique combination of assets to the work: she had enough training to read and understand the science, she was scrupulous about the details, she was by nature a synthesizer rather than a reductionist, she was a gifted writer, and she commanded, on the strength of three best-selling books, a huge audience. She was also aware, by the time she was finishing *Silent Spring*, that she was dying of cancer and that the book would certainly be her last testament; the

underlying tone of urgency in the book is one factor in its great
power. When it appeared in 1962, *Silent Spring* had a bigger impact
than Carson could ever have imagined. Although it was vigorously,
even viciously, and nearly unanimously attacked in scientific circles
as the work of an hysterical amateur, with such effectiveness that
even today it will occasionally be asserted by an environmentalist
with the stature of a Bill McKibben that Carson was not a
scientist, the book, precisely because it was scientifically sound,
held and took root. It changed attitudes not only about pesticides
but about the earth itself, and about science, and was the critical
spark that ignited the environmental movement that has endured
now for three generations.

Edward O. Wilson had the quintessential naturalist's childhood.
He grew up, that is, poor, lonely, socially an outsider. His father
was an itinerant government accountant, constantly on the move.
Wilson's elementary and secondary education took place in
fifteen or sixteen schools. During the last eight of those years, the
family moved from one city to another ten times, often lodging
in boarding houses. In the summers he was farmed out to family
friends in Alabama, Florida, Virginia, Maryland, and the District
of Columbia. He was perpetually the new kid on the block. He
was, moreover, somewhat deaf, he had blinded one eye as a young
boy when he collided with the sharp spine of a panfish, and he was
slightly built: hardly the sort of boy to make his way in the sports-
minded culture of his peers. There was no educational theory in
1938, he remarks in his autobiography, "to suggest that loneliness
in a beautiful environment might be a good if risky way to create
a scientist, at least a field biologist." There is no such educational
theory now, either, but that formula might describe the childhood

of most important naturalists in American literature. There is, I might note parenthetically, one other striking convergence in the biographies of naturalists. In nearly every instance, lurking somewhere in the background, there is an absent, or tortured, or ineffectual father. Thoreau's father was affable and inept. Muir's father prayed in his study while his boys cleared the land and ran the family farm. About Carson's father, her biographers mention only his name; there would seem to have been little else to tell. Wilson's father was alcoholic, suffered from ulcers and acute chronic bronchitis brought on by a three-pack-a-day cigarette habit, and ultimately committed suicide. I do not know what to make of this except to observe that the human consolation found in nature is among the most compelling self-interested arguments against destroying it. Wilson knew by the time he was a teenager that he wanted to spend his life as a field biologist. His monaural vision and impaired hearing ruled out birds, amphibians, and most mammals, but the sight in his good eye, it turned out, was not only undamaged but hyperacute. He was equipped to study small things. So insects it would be, he decided. Not butterflies. Too much was already known about them, and there were many excellent lepidopterists at work. Flies, he thought, would be the ideal choice: he found them beautiful, they existed everywhere in great diversity, and most of them had not yet been identified, much less studied. He sent off for the necessary supplies. But the Second World War was just beginning, Czechoslovakia's borders were already closed to international trade, and the long black mounting pins he needed were made there. He would have to settle for a subject he could collect and preserve with supplies available at the local drug store. And so it was that he became a specialist in ants. Eventually Wilson learned more about ants than any other human being, and his curiosity about them led him far beyond his nominal subject. His interest in their evolution led him to name and essentially to found the field of evolutionary biology. His interest in their patterns of distribution ultimately inspired the theory of island biogeography, one of the seminal theoretical ideas of twentieth-century biology. His interest in the social organization of ants led him to coin the word "biophilia" and to advance a theory of sociobiology, an idea that has been bitterly opposed, but mainly on ideological rather than on evidentiary grounds. His work on ants led him to the tropical rainforests of the world, with which he fell in love, and his grief over their widespread destruction prompted him, late in life, to become a social activist and, in this role, a popularizer of the idea of biodiversity, a word that did not exist fifteen years ago and which is now part of the vocabulary of every educated citizen on the planet. Despite his lifelong sinecure in an elite institution—Harvard University—and despite his path-breaking work on several frontiers of biological science, Wilson, when he recently published his autobiography, gave it the unassuming, indeed old-fashioned, title *Naturalist*. In it, he writes that he never thought of his work in any other terms, that he always wanted to be simply a discoverer, dazzled by the variety of nature and thrilled by any new discovery of even such a modest sort as the discovery of a new species of ant.

These four writers—Henry David Thoreau, John Muir, Rachel Carson, and Edward O. Wilson—span a century and a half during which science, in the contemporary sense, emerged from its infancy and developed into the primary intellectual force of our time. In terms of our assumptions about the nature of the world, Thoreau entered his adult life closer to the Paleolithic than to the twenty-first century. The rapturous writings in his journals about the railroad and the telegraph wire—he was not simple-mindedly anti-technological—reflect the fact that each was, in his lifetime, a revolutionary invention. Thoreau lived barely long enough to have heard of Darwin, and even Wilson remembers, in his autobiography, a time an astonishingly few years ago when a proposal to hire one ecologist at Harvard University was regarded as an outrageous venture into hokum. Everybody at Harvard who counted knew, as recently as the late 1970s, that the future of science lay in molecular biology and not in the study of biological systems or in the work of taxonomists like Wilson, whom his condescending colleague James Watson referred to as stamp collectors. Although these writers represent very different stages of our recent past; were as divergent in temperament as any four human beings one might choose at random; traveled, literally and figuratively, in quite different realms; and ranged in formal training from Wilson's Ivy League Ph.D. to Muir's essentially grammar school education, they shared several key intellectual qualities that illuminate not only their work but the larger role of literary natural historians in our culture. These writers were all, for one thing, generalists rather than narrow specialists. Thoreau's famous remark, "I have traveled much, in Concord," might well stand as their intellectual credo. It was not that they didn't delve deeply into their chosen subjects. Thoreau kept elaborate phenologies of the blooming of the plants in the vicinity of Concord and spent ten years assiduously tracing the dispersal of every kind of seed he could find within a day's walk of his house. Muir planted stakes in the glaciers of the Sierra Nevadas and traced

37

their movements inch by inch through many years in his effort to understand how they worked and what influence they had on the surrounding landscape. Carson may have set some kind of record for the reading of arcane journal articles in dozens of highly technical specialties. Wilson, as a young scientist, literally circled the globe in search of every kind of ant he could find. These were not merely stamp collectors. Nor is it the case that these thinkers rejected the reductionist premise of science, the notion that you can learn something valid about a whole system by examining closely its parts, the idea so central to the intellectual movement known as the Enlightenment and to the Industrial Revolution that it spawned. One argument now commonly advanced is that holism—the notion that the system rather than the individual is the basic unit of reality and that this reality embodies something larger than the sum of its parts—is a viable, indeed necessary, replacement for reductionism. The problem is, of course, that the choice—reductionism or holism—is a false choice. It is entirely probable that both points of view offer versions of the truth that are, at once, useful and, taken exclusively, misleading; that a vision of life embracing its real complexity will be neither reductionist nor holistic, but something else altogether, arrived at in the synthesis of these points of view, together with as many others as we can imagine. The task of making sense of the world does not so much lie in finding the supposedly single "correct" perspective as in learning to assimilate many perspectives, reductionism and holism among them. The obvious problem with reductionism is that it fails to account for the effects of synergy, or, as a geneticist might say, of pleiotropy. The obvious problem with holism, on the other hand, is that it fails to account for the ways in which the system itself may be radically altered by the random influence of any one of its parts. If holism alone were true, we ought to be able, by now, to predict accurately next Monday's weather. If reductionism alone were true, we ought to be able to solve the nation's crime problem by building more prisons. The genius of the four writers I am discussing is that they worked reductively—which is the only practical possibility, since no human being yet born has been able to think about the whole world all at once—but did not stop there. They were all, by temperament, despite their methods of working, synthesizers. You can tell a lot about how a clock works by taking it apart and examining its pieces, but if you never put it back together again, your knowledge will not result in a more accurate sense of time. These writers were specialists who thought to try to reassemble the pieces of their work. They had a talent for generalization and the courage to indulge in it.

They were all intellectuals, moreover, with a democratic temperament. They assumed their ideas could and ought to be communicated to a general audience. Even Wilson, when he sat down to write an encyclopedic survey of all that is known about ants, a subject one would hardly think suitable for wide dissemination, took such care with his work and wrote so accessibly that the resulting volume won a Pulitzer Prize in literature. These were not writers to hide in thickets of jargon, or to be content with publishing their ideas in places where only their colleagues would be likely to see them. They did not mistake obscurity of expression for depth of vision. In a time when scientific information is increasingly offered as an exclusive substitute not only for other kinds of learning but also for any conversation that is not strictly technical, these writers made

a principled effort to include citizens at large in the discussion
and provoked widespread debate about issues of science and
technology. A long line of critics, especially of literary critics who
have been bored with his interest in nature, have painted Thoreau
as a cranky misogynist who advocated that everybody retire to
a hermitage, but the central question he raised remains urgently
relevant: what, he asked, is the relationship between technological
(or material) advancement and human happiness, and what would
be required for the former to enhance the latter? Muir was the
first, and in some ways is still the loudest, critic of the U.S. Forest
Service's multiple use policy. Are there, he asked, any long-term
values in nature that transcend their short-term exploitation?
Carson raised the central power question: can nature be
overwhelmed, she asked, or must it be accommodated? What sort
of victory, she asked, can we expect from a war with nature? What,
Wilson asks, is the relationship between nature and culture?
Both have co-evolved through at least the last ten thousand years.
Would it be helpful to know how each has influenced the other?
These are serious questions with profound consequences for the
planet's future, and not one of them can be answered by resort
to technicalities alone. Not one of these questions would yield a
publishable article in a refereed scientific journal, although much
that is published in such journals could shed some light on the
possibilities. They are questions that overreach the limits of the
demonstrable. One challenge that these writers pose is whether we
can afford a system of scholarship that, at its highest levels, actively
discourages asking the biggest questions. Particularly with respect
to technology, we now frequently face that conundrum in which
technologists disavow responsibility for the social consequences

of their inquiries and inventions, claiming, quite properly, that such matters ought to be discussed by society as a whole, while at the same time communicating their own knowledge in language unintelligible, in many cases, even to other scientists outside their specialties and, at the same time, branding anybody who sees any negative implication in their work as unscientific, or Luddite, or a threat to the freedom of scientific inquiry. Rachel Carson's challenge to the indiscriminate use of certain kinds of pesticides was not generally answered in the scientific community with countervailing scientific evidence but by just such ad hominen attacks. Were it not for the intervention of scientifically literate thinkers like Carson, whose fates are independent of their curricula vitae, we might be obliged to accept all scientific and technological developments on faith, just as the medieval faithful, deprived of the Bible in the vernacular, were obliged to accept all theology as divinely inspired. The natural historians, in our culture, have been the democratizers of science and technology.

They have been, as well, the keepers of the pre-Enlightenment idea that, in the largest sense, there is only one earth history, and that is natural history. For a time we were inclined to forget that, although we are creatures of culture, and culture is an artifact of the mind, the mind itself is a biological organ, and that we cannot, therefore, escape our common heritage with the rest of life. Death is nature's way of reminding us that we are, after all, creatures and not gods. There is a wonderful Blackfeet myth that expresses this truth. In the beginning, in the Blackfeet story of the creation, as in so many accounts of the origins of life on earth, including the modern scientific one, there was water. One day Old Man decided to find out what lay beneath the water. So he sent down

41

diving animals on reconnaissance: a duck, an otter, a beaver, a badger; they all dived in vain. Then he sent down a muskrat, which returned with a lump of mud in its paws. When the Old Man blew upon it, the mud swelled up until it became the earth. Old Man traveled the length and breadth of the new earth, piling up stones to make mountains, digging rivers and lakes and filling them with water, creating grasses to cover the prairies, and trees to shade the forests, and birds and animals of every kind. Then he made for himself a wife, Old Woman, who was very clever. The two of them decided together how people should be made. Old Man insisted on having first say in everything, which Old Woman agreed to, so long as she could have last say. People should have eyes and mouths, arranged vertically on their faces, Old Man said. Fine, said his wife, but they should be situated crosswise. They should have ten fingers on each hand. Fingers they shall have, Old Woman said, but so many would be awkward; let people have four fingers and a thumb on each hand. Then came the big question: should they live forever or should people die? "I'll toss a buffalo chip on the water," Old Man said. "If it floats, people shall die four days and then rise again. If it sinks, people shall die."

"As you wish," Old Woman said, "but let me toss a stone into the water instead." The stone, of course, sank, and so it was decided that people should die. Old Man and Old Woman agreed that this was for the best. If they should never die, they said, then people would never feel sorry for one another.

The great contemporary oceanographer Sylvia Earle suggests another context in which our own history might be understood. If the history of the earth were to be represented, she says, on a scale equal to the depth of the deepest ocean, human civilization would occur only in the last inch, equal to the depression a floating gull makes on the surface of the sea. By insisting, through a long moment of hubris, on the reality that human history is a branch of natural history, the literary natural historians have been nurturers and preservers of the very possibility of history.

These writers also share in a refusal to acknowledge the distinction, alive since the Age of Enlightenment, between the sciences and the humanities. The extremes are best represented by Thoreau, whose apprenticeship was as a poet, and Wilson, whose earliest interests were exclusively scientific. Thoreau worried in his journal that his poetry would be overwhelmed by his science. He thought science, in itself, a barren enterprise, but he thought poetry written on instinct alone equally so. "At first blush," he said, "a man is not capable of reporting truth; he must be drenched and saturated with it first. What was enthusiasm in the young man must become temperament in the mature man. Without excitement, heat, or passion, he will survey the world which excited the youth and threw him off his balance…. A style in which matter is all in all, and the manner nothing at all." Thoreau insisted, like a good scientist, that a writer's work ought to be founded upon facts, but, more than that, upon such facts as the writer has had occasion personally to verify. He also insisted, like a good humanitarian, indeed like a good deconstructionist humanitarian, that those facts were useless until they had been established in some context that revealed their significance. "Facts," he wrote in his journal, "should be only as the frame to my pictures; … facts to tell who I am, and where I have been or what I have thought; as now the bell rings for the evening meeting, and its volumes of sound, like smoke which rises where a cannon is fired, make the tent in which

I dwell. My facts shall be falsehood to the common sense. I should so state the facts that they shall be significant, shall be myths or mythologic." We now assume, tragically—for myths are among the highest expressions of the human imagination—that myths are by definition false, but what Thoreau was talking about, in essence, was the social construction of reality, which he believed to be of a higher order of truth than the mere facts. Here Thoreau predicts, as he foreshadowed so many ideas in our culture, Foucault. Wilson writes in his autobiography about being powerfully impressed as an undergraduate student by Erwin Schrödinger's *What is Life?*, which argued that it is nothing more than a physical process, entirely explicable by the laws of physics and chemistry; and by Ernst Mayr's *Systematics and the Origin of Species*, which offered a keystone synthesis of genetics and evolutionary theory. For Wilson, "Science became the new light and the way." Still, he remembered that he had experienced a Christian conversion only three years earlier. "Religion, I knew from personal experience," he writes, "is a perpetual fountainhead of human emotion. It cannot be dismissed as superstition. It cannot be compartmentalized as the manifestation of some separate world. From the beginning I could never accept that science and religion are separate domains, with fundamentally different questions and answers. This, Wilson says, looking back on a lifetime of science, is still the view he holds. And it has been, in general, the view of the literary natural historians, who have always walked with one foot in science and the other in the humanities, unwilling to relinquish either, valuing both for their revealing disparities of method, but refusing to see them as concerned with fundamentally different questions and answers. Current trends in literary theory, in particular, apply self-consciously scientific models to the methods of the humanities, threatening to make even the arts into subjects so arcane, rarified, and specialized as to preclude the legitimate interest of ordinary human beings. It may well happen, if this movement continues to flourish, that, just as the writers I have been discussing have kept history alive, so their successors will preserve what used to be thought of as the humanities, rather as monks copied out the classical texts in anticipation of the Renaissance, against that dark time when we will have specialized ourselves into utter incoherence.

I would, finally, mark this about the literary natural historians: they are all, to the last one, celebrants of wonder. There is not a cynic in the lot. "A child's world," Rachel Carson wrote, "is fresh and new and beautiful, full of wonder and excitement. It is our misfortune that for most of us that clear-eyed vision, that true instinct for what is beautiful and awe-inspiring, is dimmed and even lost before we reach adulthood. If I had influence with the good fairy who is supposed to preside over the christening of all children, I should ask that her gift to each child in the world be a sense of wonder so indestructible that it would last throughout life, as an unfailing antidote against the boredom and disenchantment of later years, the sterile preoccupation with things that are artificial, the alienation from our sources of strength." Good science in our time is anti-mystical, and good humanities scholarship is anti-romantic. We fear above all else, as scholars, that we might be caught in an unguarded moment of sentiment or nostalgia. The great sin of our age is to think fondly of the past. But in the world of the gene, in our biology, we are inextricably bound to the very beginnings of life. To despise the past, therefore—to suppose that our highest intellectual goal is to debunk all that has gone before us—is to despise ourselves. There is no higher or miserable arrogance than that which denies our beginnings. To wonder, to be astonished, to feel awe, is the beginning of a suitable humility. "Whatever attitude to human existence you fashion for yourself, know that it is valid only if it be the shadow of an attitude to Nature," Henry Beston wrote. His words might serve to summarize this whole intellectual tradition. "A human life," he wrote, "so often likened to a spectacle upon a stage, is more justly a ritual. The ancient values of dignity, beauty, and poetry which sustain it are of Nature's inspiration; they are born of the mystery and beauty of the world. Do no dishonour to the earth lest you dishonour the spirit of man. Hold your hands out over the earth as over a flame. To all who love her, who open to her the doors of their veins, she gives of her strength, sustaining them with her own tremor of dark life. Touch the earth, love the earth, honour the earth, her plains, her valleys, her hills, and her seas; rest your spirit in her solitary places. For the gifts of life are the earth's and they are given to all, and they are the songs of birds at daybreak, Orion and the Bear, and dawn seen over ocean from the beach."

Ecology and Memory:
The Essays of Paul Gruchow

Louis Martinelli

O bird on the green branch of the dying tree…
Sing me toward home…
— Thomas McGrath
Letter to an Imaginary Friend: Part I

I remember the first time I heard Paul Gruchow's voice.

He was being interviewed on public radio, his subject the North American tallgrass prairie. The voice I heard was eloquent, persuasive and lyrical—qualities I was soon to find in his essays. It was an original and startlingly intelligent voice. I felt that I had been waiting to hear it for a long time: a native of the Midwest passionately making connections between present and past, exposing the distance between our environmental rhetoric and the reality of our policies and lives, exploring in personal terms the relationship between damage and healing. What I heard was a regional writer with a gift for telling the story of ecology, which is the story of particular places.

In his first book, *Journal of a Prairie Year*, Gruchow begins by telling us the experience of the prairie is one of "immensity" and "immersion." "The essential feature of the prairie," he insists, "is its horizon, which you can neither walk to nor touch. It is like the horizon of the sea" (x). The scale of the prairie is so large it cannot be adequately photographed. "The experience," he declares, "is a kind of baptism" (x). But immersion reveals a tragedy: the integrity of the prairie ecosystem—its capacity for sustaining an underground forest of roots twenty-five miles long for every square meter of sod—has been violated. On a 600-mile drive from Winnipeg, Manitoba, Canada to Worthington, Minnesota, Gruchow cannot find any land that has not been turned over "furrow by furrow" (xi).

Baptism will lead to pilgrimage in *Journal of a Prairie Year* and in all the books to follow. Sometimes the direction is backward in time to the wonder and pain of a boyhood farm in western Minnesota. Sometimes the journey involves leaving human communities in order to walk or canoe into wilderness. Always there is a return to the writing desk, followed by another pilgrimage back to nature:

> I had come to the lake because I had been writing about
> it for days, and the more I wrote about it, the less I could
> remember it. To write about something is to take leave
> of it. I needed to find my sense of the lake again. (24)

In all these journeys, the damaged tallgrass prairie and Gruchow's agricultural roots will not be forgotten.

In speaking of Thomas McGrath, perhaps the greatest poet of the Northern Plains, Dale Jacobsen cites McGrath's *Letter to an Imaginary Friend* as an example of what he calls "circularity." For McGrath, the boundaries separating past, present and future, inner and outer, merge until time itself becomes a circle. Circularity is, for McGrath, the ambiguity we have inherited from nature and history. A repetition can be a comforting rhythm to fall asleep by, such as the night rain, or it can be a curse, as when soil erosion or domestic abuse becomes intergenerational (409-413).

Circularity has been important in Native American tribes and is found in many peasant cultures as well. In his historical novel *Pig Earth*, John Berger explains how a French peasant's life is committed almost completely to survival. The peasantry everywhere can be defined as a class of survivors. And yet, for the first time in history, the survivors may not survive, for the culture worshipping progress is a straight road envisioning only future expansion, while the culture of survival envisages a circle of repeated acts. Any transformation a peasant imagines, Berger says, involves his becoming again the peasant he once was. Berger contrasts the culture of the peasant—uninsulated, open to seasonal changes or the natural process of aging—to that of the urban twentieth-century consumer, living in a suffocating, over-serviced limbo. If the urban planners have their way, Berger warned twenty-five years ago, there will be no more peasants (196 ff.).

Paul Gruchow was born in the middle of the twentieth century into the American equivalent of peasant culture. In *Journal of a Prairie Year*, the paradox of circularity is everywhere, growing directly out of the author's childhood. Remembering his grandfather's death when he was four, Gruchow recalls sitting next to the corpse, "nauseated by the scent of flowers and of body perfume":

> We waited a very long time in that parlor, and the odors of the place grew as we sat there, waiting, I suppose, for condolences to be said. The room grew cloyingly hot. There was a tropical steaminess about it. But when we went to bury my grandfather, we encountered a bitter wind, and the snow was running again. For a long time after that, I smelled the odor of death in the snow winds. (25)

Writing, in part, "the history of my home place," Gruchow points out how it had to be settled twice. From 1874 to 1878, swarms of Rocky Mountain locusts came, chewing their way across the land, eating everything in sight: grass, corn, the grain in the bin, handles of pitchforks, the sills off the windows, even the harnesses of horses standing in the yard. Visiting the schoolhouse of his youth, Gruchow finds it gone, a cornfield in its place, "and all the corn in it was dead and dying." The church, still standing, was no longer used for worship, the parsonage boarded up. Finally, the grieving pilgrim finds the graves of his parents: "My tears…were a kind of benediction: something wet in the midst of all that thirst" (75).

These themes—circularity, memory and its ambiguity, going away and coming home—are taken up again in *Grass Roots: The Universe of Home*. In seventeen essays, Gruchow argues for a return to nostalgia, defined in terms of its Greek etymological root as both a literal and metaphorical going home. In a wide-ranging collection that is deeply personal and fiercely persuasive, I hesitate to single out two individual essays for virtuosity, but "The Transfiguration of Bread" and "What We Teach Rural Children" are such masterful expressions of the book's themes, they invite praise.

"One evening when one thing after another had gone wrong, Mother opened the cupboard door and a dinner plate crashed to the floor and shattered" (41). From that ominous beginning, the monetary impoverishment of a struggling family is contrasted with the richness of their farm and its household. Homemade bread is offered as the symbol and sustenance of grass roots' wealth. When the Gruchow children left their small local school as adolescents and entered a large consolidated town school, hunger for their mother's bread was replaced by shame: "We had acquired the preference of the age for anything manufactured over anything homemade. We suddenly coveted boughten bread.…We were no longer content to eat hick bread" (45-6). When Gruchow's mother finally gave up making bread and began to buy a factory-made substitute, the triumph of industrialized farming over agriculture had begun in earnest: "The wholesome mystery of bread, the sacrament of it…was never in the ingredients but in the labor, and in the laborers who transfigured them into bread" (47).

"The Bread of This World" is the title of a wonderful, not well-enough known poem by Thomas McGrath. Gruchow's essay can stand as a fitting complement to McGrath's eloquent verse in which "The holy loaves of the bread are slowly being born/rising like low hills in the steepled pastures of light/Lifting the prairie farmhouse afternoon on their arching backs" (*Selected Poems* 100).

"What We Teach Rural Children" is surely a tour-de-force among essays which argue against what Wendell Berry has called the unsettling of America through displacement of small farmers and debasement of local economy and culture. Gruchow's essay pivots on an exploration of class in America and on a critique of stereotypical thinking that reduces white rural people to a homogenous glob. In his view, the denigration of rural people proceeds from the denial that they are an underclass and from the assumption that they are all alike. In schools, rural children are taught as a matter of course "that opportunity of every kind lies elsewhere" (91), and the failure and decline of rural culture are the fault of parents and grandparents. What we impose upon rural children, then, is "a kind of homelessness" (100). Speaking from his own experience, Gruchow articulates the hidden and not-so-hidden message of rural education: "If you're any good you go somewhere else." And we know the cutting edge of that displacement as rural people continue their half-century of migration toward so-called bigger and better places.

The Grace of Grass & Water

It is instructive to follow the progression of thought from these two seminal essays through "What Time Is It?," in which the term "postmodern" is declared to be nonsense, a double negative negating the future by disavowing the past: "It is, of course, the logical extension of recent intellectual history. In this century God was declared dead, and then history followed. The death of time was only a matter of time" (141).

In "Visions," the narrative voice returns to evoke the author's boyhood bedroom, speculating about the nature of what can be seen in the world and what lies just beyond. In this breathtaking passage, Gruchow is at his lyrical best:

> And then the hour before dawn arrived, crisp and
> clear, the breathless hour when even the animals seem
> to pause and ponder, the universal hour of reverie.
> A golden halo of light bathed the grassy ridge tops,
> but the forest and the river were still cast in heavy
> shadow. Our sleeping bags were covered with frost, and
> inside them we were lightly dressed. We awaited the
> benediction of the sun. (174)

In "Bones," *Grass Roots'* concluding essay, Grandfather Gruchow's embalmed body and burial are invoked a second time, death and wildness reconnected, and salvation found in "the ancient cries of gray wolves" (205). The voice here is nostalgic in the best possible sense: the past is not allowed to become an object of sentimentality but is made to live again in the present. The miracle of a bone, we learn, is that it is evidence of something "never to be repeated, that has vanished yet nevertheless endures in bone, a faint white glimmering, in some offhand place, of life everlasting" (209).

Is this not the transcendentalism of Emerson and Thoreau?

If *Journal of a Prairie Year* and *Grass Roots: The Universe of Home* can be thought of as explorations of domestic order and the reconstruction, through memory, of our damaged prairie ecology, then Gruchow's *The Necessity of Empty Places* and *Boundary Waters: The Grace of the Wild* might be seen as a passing over into an ecology that largely survives, but is vulnerable. Like Aldo Leopold, his conservationist mentor, Gruchow shows how, in empty places, human observation, experience, and consciousness are the cornerstones of any viable land ethic. "A mountain is a perception," he reminds us, "as much as anything" (*Necessity* 5). And so begins a pilgrimage through the "Blue Mountains" of Minnesota, the Nebraska Sandhills, Wyoming's Big Horn Basin, and the Beartooth Range of Montana.

It is in the Big Horns that Gruchow begins to be aware of the nature and value of emptiness. He and his hiking partner John Scholl are headed toward Florence Canyon and the Cloud Peak Primitive Area when they discover they are in "houseless, roadless, trailless places… In a sense they were always empty. The places that survive now as wilderness are by nature demanding, uncompromising, parsimonious" (73). It is these qualities Gruchow will find in what our culture has taught most of us to fear and avoid experiencing at all cost, "the void within ourselves, the loneliness, the surviving heart of wildness, that binds us to all the living earth" (75). It is as if the spiritual journeying of the hermetic mystics of the twelfth century has found its twentieth-century equivalent in a backpacker.

Although this is not a how-to-do-it manual, there is advice here about a kind of inner discipline in the wilderness that runs counter to the tourist's preoccupation with the quick and scenic. Gruchow urges us to walk slowly, quoting Colin Fletcher's rule governing pace: "slow and slower." Gruchow tells us the right tempo is one that allows for conversation and natural breathing: "The right stride returns instinctively to a walker because it is as metrical and regular as the rhythm of a song" (78).

Commenting on the rising and setting of the sun on the plains, he compares them to a Passion play, with alternating rhythms of death and resurrection. In the mountains, "at any moment the sun may precipitously disappear, may retreat behind a mountain, never to return, as if giving way without a struggle to the night. The difference is that night on the plains descends from the heavens and in the deep valleys of the mountains it arises from the earth" (84-85).

Perhaps the finest chapter in *The Necessity of Empty Places*, "Medicine Mountain" is a meditation on the idea of holy places. Inspired by the Medicine Wheel, an early Native American stone construction, Gruchow reflects on research suggesting the only historical certainty about the twenty-eight-spoked, seven-cairned wheel is the fact that its story has vanished. Walking alone, honoring the speechlessness which "begins awe for life," the pilgrim comes to a deeper understanding of the void as he looks beyond the visible world of the Big Horn and its basin. He feels diminished from such a height and tells us this is good. Echoing Albert Schweitzer, he argues that humility is the beginning of reverence for life.

"The error of earlier ethics," Schweitzer believed, "is that it conceived itself as concerned only with the relations of man to man. The real question is, however, one concerning man's relations to the world and all which comes within his reach. A man is ethical only when life as such is holy to him, that is, the lives of plants and animals as well as the lives of men." And Schweitzer adds an important and overlooked sentence: "The ethics of reverence for life includes all that can be called love, devotion, compassion, joy and endeavor" (88).

Not surprisingly, Gruchow embraces all of these essentially human qualities on his journey through empty places, returning to Western Minnesota a more conscious, home-loving person.

Of his published books, *Boundary Waters: The Grace of the Wild* is Gruchow's most critically acclaimed. Mary Pipher called it "our twentieth-century *Walden*." Writing in *The Bloomsbury Review*, critic Abigail Davis described it as "a book of marvelous depth and diversity...Gruchow's best in a long history of excellent work."

The book's central essay, "The Grace of the Wild," recounts in rich and exalted prose the author's summer "travels in canoe country," the title of a previously published photo essay in collaboration with the photographer Gerald Brimacombe in which the text of "The Grace of the Wild" originally appeared. The essay is not harmed from its publication without the excellent photographs of the earlier coffee-table book. Gruchow's prose is colorful enough to command our attention as he evokes lakes, rocks, campsites and native pictographs in all their changing mood and detail. The essay continues the meditative tone of *The Necessity of Empty Places*, even incorporating a monastic prayer schedule (morning lauds to late-night compline) as its formal structure.

Gruchow's descriptive powers have few peers among contemporary essayists, and here the lyrical quality of his language approaches that of our finest prose poets:

> Faintly at first, like a whisper of wind, I hear the sound of running water. As I approach it, its language becomes more distinct, the babble of many voices in an unfamiliar language. And then I am upon the rapids, the water slipping over stones like liquid silk, its voice now a low murmur, the sound of an astonished crowd. (32)

There are too many passages the equal of this one to quote liberally. One simply has to read them aloud to appreciate the finely chiseled language and its music.

The Boundary Waters being traveled, of course, is the Quetico-Superior Wilderness, a two-and-a-half-million-acre tract lying on each side of the line separating Minnesota and Canada. As Gruchow points out in his preface, he means also to include the whole region stretching from the northern inland lakes to Lake Superior and Isle Royale in his exploration. In fall the canoe is forsaken for foot travel, and Gruchow is reunited with John Scholl, his hiking partner. Their trek will proceed across the northeastern corner of the Boundary Waters, then follow the Minnesota-Ontario border to Fort Charlotte on the Pigeon River, and finally descend the arduous Grand Portage trail to Lake Superior. "This is canoe country," the author informs us, "but, despite my bum knees, we mean to walk" (75).

And walk they do. It is the most difficult of all the hikes Gruchow chronicles in his books, in large part because of the uneven, demanding terrain. This is, after all, *canoe* country. The last part of the trail, once endured by French voyageurs carrying hundred-pound parcels the whole seven-mile length, I personally remember as a slow descent through hell: clouds of mosquitoes, biting flies, jagged rocks of such size and angularity they in no way resemble a staircase. The border trail, if it can be called a trail, is a kind of *via negativa* of the body and soul, a test of spiritual will. For Gruchow, perhaps, that is the point: not the postcard sunsets on the lake or predictable comforts of the resorts that dot the northern landscape. "The road is long and difficult," said the mystic St. John of the Cross (55). There is a dark night in which the soul finally awakens—and it is out of reach for tourists.

The border trail and its wrong turns, a lost rope needed to tie up food and elevate it beyond the reach of bears, an early winter, the scalding of an arm when a tree stump proves to be an unsteady table, fourteen-hour hiking days, middle-aged knees, the refusal of the ground to be level at night—all of these travails seem to be background for another, more subtle theme: friendship. Friendship, we should recall, was Plato's enduring concern as a philosopher. It is, not coincidentally, the concern of the poet McGrath, the conservationist Leopold, and the humanitarian Schweitzer. We take as a truism of the modern world that "no man is an island"—even our greeting cards are variations on this theme—but we struggle to believe it. Most of us believe ourselves to be too sophisticated to wait on our personal islands for messages in bottles, but we accept confirmation of our relational natures by e-mail. Most of us feel we don't have time to cultivate the leisure Plato argued is a condition of friendship. But in the wilderness, Gruchow reminds us, there is all the time in the world if the traveler goes on foot, goes light, and is willing to be lost, at least some of the time.

Many of the best passages in "Walking the Border," as in
other accounts of trips gone awry, involve the impact being lost
has on friendship: how it strains and tests the hikers, calling for
greater patience than either normally possesses; how ultimately it
strengthens and deepens their mutual respect. Not surprisingly,
in Gruchow's work, friendship, family, community, and nature
are of a piece. What is important are the connections, never to
be forgotten, between these graceful and ultimately mysterious
realities. What is required is the willingness to be opened by
uncertainty and, as Plato would affirm, to realize we share our
ignorance with other human beings.

"Think of our life in nature," Thoreau tells us. "Who are we?
Where are we?" (*Maine Woods* 95). We do not know. And that is
the point.

In "By Light of the Winter Moon," three college students
reading *Walden* and Gruchow, their instructor, decide to try a
North Woods version of Thoreau's experiment. In dead of winter,
they will stay in a log cabin near the end of the Gunflint Trail in
the heart of Minnesota canoe country. There may be no more exact
description of light in Northern literature than Gruchow reflecting
on the light a full moon casts on snow, which he calls "the most
beautiful light in the world":

> Its glow seems to emanate not from the heavens but
> from within the earth and to radiate out into the
> darkness of space. The second most beautiful light in
> the world is the light of the midday sun on snow, light
> at its most transparent....Sunlight on snow sparkles;
> moonlight shimmers on it. Winter days are naked;
> winter nights are veiled in blue lace and sequins. (122-23)

Cross-country skiing on a snowmobile trail over a frozen snow-covered lake and leading his students into an experiential form of learning to support the discussion of *Walden*, Gruchow returns to the idea of friendship:

> And the landscape conveyed a strange aura of intimacy.
> Vastness, emptiness, austerity have the paradoxical
> effect of opening up the self, of rendering it vulnerable
> to the persuasions of the heart. Noise, busyness, bustle,
> abundance—the trappings of industrial life—are
> enemies of intimacy. Is it any wonder that our industrial
> lives are so violent? (126)

Violence, of course, is the enemy of friendship, community its foundation and true home.

One of the stories within this story is that of James, a difficult student, who is led from anxiety and withdrawal to an appreciation of wildness. The group experience, coupled with the surrounding wilderness, gradually draws him in as Gruchow masterfully weaves a parable about the power of nature to transform both teacher and learner—education's forgotten purpose. Finally, the author as teacher realizes several years later that he had failed his own course by failing to recognize how "there was a wilderness in my study, and in my kitchen, and in my bedroom…if only I had the alertness to discern it" (157).

In *Boundary Waters'* last essay, "Wild Isle," the unique environmental balances of Lake Superior's Isle Royale, which once included wolves and moose, are explored on foot after a harrowing ferry ride across choppy water. There are wonderful descriptions of animals encountered on the trail—most memorably a moose at Washington Creek—and information about the island's natural history and topography. Gruchow ends by recalling the distinction Thoreau made between "wilderness," which is limited to a specific geographical and ecological space, and "wildness," which is the nature in and all around us. Remembering through self-hypnosis his surprise encounter with the moose, Gruchow tells us he has returned to Isle Royale many times without leaving his reading chair: "When I go there, I retreat into the wildness of my own brain, transcending the limits of living in a world of words or of my own kind alone and reveling in the grace of the wild" (202).

In addition to the four published books discussed here, Gruchow's work includes a collection of essays first published in *Minnesota Conservation Volunteer*, a DNR magazine, that explore Minnesota's scientific and natural area preserves. Appropriately named *Worlds within a World*, the book and its subjects range from a Root River bluffside goat prairie to an old-growth forest, Lutsen Woods, above Lake Superior. The book is handsomely illustrated by photographs, the majority of them taken by Minnesota native John Gregor.

At the time of Gruchow's tragic suicide in February, 2004, at age 56, there were dozens of uncollected essays, lectures, critical book reviews, tape recordings, book forewords, and at least one unpublished manuscript—a gripping, soul-baring memoir which explores his struggles with childhood abuse, major depression, and the failure of the mental health treatment system to help him. "The Meaning of Natural History," reprinted in the collection you are now reading, is a more conceptual work, arguing for an understanding of Earth's history as being synonymous with natural history. In support of this idea, Gruchow cites the work of

Henry David Thoreau, John Muir, Rachel Carson, and Edward O. Wilson in affirming our commonality with all of life.

How are we to assess the importance of this considerable body of literary work?

I suggested earlier that Gruchow's voice is eloquent, persuasive, and lyrical. I have said that ecology—the greatest metaphor of the twentieth century—and memory—the foundation of human culture—are inseparable in his writing. I have compared him to the Great Plains poet Thomas McGrath, seeing an awareness of circularity, a pattern of leaving and returning home, in each author's writing. His own words, "There is no death so final as the death of a memory," could serve as a motto, it seems to me, for a Paul Gruchow reader.

"What anthropologists distinguish as cultures," Ivan Illich writes, "the historian of mental spaces might distinguish as different memories." For Gruchow's essays to be of enduring value and excellence, we must leave them believing our damaged ecologies—the places where we live—can be made whole in part by remembering them when they were whole, then living in such a way as to restore them. We must come to a deeper understanding of ecology itself: that it is metaphor more than science, the remembered and passed-on story of individual places. And how, for Paul Gruchow, this remembering and telling becomes, at its best, song.

Jane Hirshfield, musing on the nature of poetry, calls it "language put into the forms of remembrance." Quoting Yeats— "The friends that have it I do wrong/whenever I remake a song/ Should know what issue is at stake:/it is myself that I remake"

(16)—she might well be describing the accomplishment of the deep ecologist whose method is the art of the personal essay.

One of the highest compliments that can be paid a writer is to say that his or her work continues a heritage, a tradition of similarly important work. When I think of our twentieth-century essayists and poets of place—of John Muir and Aldo Leopold, of Wendell Berry and Gary Snyder, of Thomas McGrath and Mary Oliver—I see how Paul Gruchow's work has been nourished by and helps continue this succession.

As we begin a new century and millennium, desperately needing to see, as Martin Heidegger has written, that "we have forgotten that we have forgotten" (qtd. in Schmitt 5, 11), I am grateful for the journeys, the lifelong pilgrimage of Paul Gruchow. When I head to the restorative silence of the wilderness or retreat to the wildness within my own house, I will take him with me.

Published Books by Paul Gruchow (in chronological order)

Journal of a Prairie Year. Minneapolis: University of Minnesota Press, 1985.

The Necessity of Empty Places. New York: St. Martin's Press, 1988. Rpt. Minneapolis: Milkweed Editions, 1999, with a new preface by Gruchow.

Travels in Canoe Country. Photographs by Gerald Brimacombe. Boston: Little, Brown and Company, 1992.

Grass Roots: The Universe of Home. Minneapolis: Milkweed Editions, 1995.

Boundary Waters: The Grace of the Wild. Minneapolis: Milkweed Editions, 1997.

Worlds within a World: Reflections on Visits to Minnesota Scientific and Natural Area Preserves. St. Paul: Minnesota Department of Natural Resources, 1999.

Other Works Cited

Berger, John. *Pig Earth*. New York: Chatto and Windus, 1992.

Davis, Abigail. "Understanding Our Limits: A Profile of Paul Gruchow." *The Bloomsbury Review*, March/April, 1988, pg.19

Fletcher, Colin. *The Man Who Walked through Time*. New York: Knopf, 1979.

Hirshfield, Jane. *Nine Gates: Entering the Mind of Poetry*. New York: Harper Collins, 1997.

Illich, Ivan. *In the Vineyard of the Text*. Chicago: University of Chicago Press, 1993.

Leopold, Aldo. *A Sand County Almanac and Sketches Here and There*. New York: Oxford University Press, 1949.

McGrath, Thomas. *Letters to an Imaginary Friend*. Port Townsend, WA: Copper Canyon Press, 1997.

—. *Selected Poems*. Port Townsend WA: Copper Canyon Press, 1988.

St. John of the Cross. *The Poems of St. John of the Cross*. New York: Harcourt, Brace and Company, 1999.

Schmitt, Richard. *Martin Heidegger on Being Human: Being and Time*. New York: Random House, 1969.

Schweitzer, Albert. *Pilgrimage to Humanity*. New York: The Philosophical Library, 1961.

Thoreau, Henry David. *The Maine Woods*. New York: Harper and Row, 1987.

—. *Walden and Civil Disobedience*. New York: W. W. Norton, 1966.

Louis Martinelli is a poet, playwright, essayist and educator. His play *Take My Hand* won an NEA Outstanding Achievement Award, and he has been nominated for a MacArthur Foundation "Genius Award" for his work in helping create sustainable communities. The literary executor of Paul Gruchow's estate, he is the executive director of The Paul Gruchow Foundation—a Minnesota-based non-profit organization whose mission is to foster awareness of the relationship between nature, creativity, community and mental health. A native of Cincinnati, Louis divides his time between Ohio and Minnesota—his "second home."

The Grace of Grass & Water

The Sound of
Sandhill Cranes

Mary Pipher

My friendship with Paul commenced in the early 1990s in Marshall, Minnesota, where I first heard him talk at a writers' conference. Trembling, soft-spoken, and emanating intensity, he spoke of his rural upbringing and his first close friends—Dickens, Poe, Melville, Thackeray, Cather and Thoreau. He whispered their names to underscore how sacred these writers were to him. Listening to Paul, I felt that we were the same person and that his best friends were my best friends, too.

The first book I read by Paul was *The Necessity of Empty Places*. I read it slowly, often setting it aside to ponder his beautiful writing and profound ideas. Paul's point of view on the universe broadened my thinking about the natural world. I developed a better set of eyes, eyes that noticed the exoskeleton of a cicada or the first greening of prairie grass. I acquired more sophisticated ears, ears that could hear the sandhill cranes on the Platte River in a new way, in Paul's way. He wrote, "The sound of the sandhill cranes is like the roaring of the sea in a conch shell; when you have finally heard it, you recognize that you have always known it. It is like the cry of a loon or the howl of wolves or the warning rattle of a snake, an article in the universal language" (15).

Imbibing Paul's writing, I developed an increased capacity for awe. Watching the Northern Lights or looking at maples on a blue-sky October day, I had experienced wonder. Yet Paul helped me respond to smaller beauties—a ribbon on the wire fence at Medicine Wheel, a tuft of prairie grass, or the pattern of ice in an old bucket. He taught me to watch for ouzels near waterfalls and to pay attention to the bugs.

Paul is responsible for some of my husband's and my happiest hours. He launched our backpacking adventures. After reading *The*

Necessity of Empty Places, we bought gear and retraced Paul's route from the Platte all the way to the Big Horn Mountains. For the first time in our lives, we slept miles from a road or any other human beings.

In our decade of friendship, Paul and I were together fewer than a dozen times, and some years passed without any contact. Yet the hours we spent together in no way reflect the significance of our friendship. I have been with people all my life who had less impact on how I view the world.

Paul was an amazing raconteur. He slept outside over one hundred nights in one year and enjoyed many adventures. No one could tell grizzly bear and rattlesnake stories like Paul could. He had a quiet, gentle sense of humor that now and then would explode into infectious hee-hee-hee's.

Everything touched Paul deeply. He had such precise and complicated memories of his own experiences. His inner landscape was vast and tangled, and his adventures were extraordinary and constant; and when he shared them in story form, they were spellbinding. Paul was a natural teacher who expected a great deal of himself and his students. For that matter, Paul expected a great deal of every moment.

As a friend, Paul was amazing and exasperating. He wasn't much for keeping in touch, but when he did show up in my town, we could talk for six hours straight about the most intimate details of our lives. Generally, he was miserable when he wasn't elated. Rarely was he able to find a safe, calm place to rest. He could not find solace in that home we ordinary mortals call contentment.

When we talked, Paul would pour out his woes and then strenuously object to all my opinions or advice. Sometimes I felt he was rather too involved with his despair and alienation, but then he embraced his elation as well. Paul was constructed in a way that never allowed him to stop taking in the world. He was always awake and in flames. Minute by minute, he faced an exquisite and terrible place, as complicated as Shakespeare's universe, with little more to protect himself than a cigarette and a pencil.

I last talked to Paul in 1997 when he came to Lincoln to receive an award from the Loren Eiseley Society. He had been in a mental hospital for many months, but, at the time he came to Lincoln, he was living in a halfway house for psychiatric patients. His doctor granted him a pass to come to Lincoln, provided he stay with Jim and me.

Saturday night in early October, Jim was working as a musician, and Paul and I drove to the university natural history museum. As we walked into the auditorium, snow was falling on trees still heavy with green leaves. That night Paul spoke on the three great influences of his life—the natural world, books, and mental illness. He told the audience he would be returning to the halfway house after the speech. He said he was on suicide watch and that, in fact, he was quite sure he would soon kill himself.

The audience of mild-mannered intellectuals, united by their love of Eiseley's writing, was stunned but also deeply moved by his words. So rarely in America does anyone just stand up in front of a crowd and tell the unadorned truth. No one who was present for that talk could ever forget it.

After the event, Paul and I drove towards my house through a howling blizzard. All around us, branches were snapping with the weight of wet snow. Tree limbs blocked the streets, and we had trouble making it home. When we arrived, I built a fire and made tea, and we talked for hours about doctors, mental hospitals, medicines, and diagnoses; the latter topic was one that Paul liked more than I did.

Paul said he had never felt more alive than he did at the halfway house. He enjoyed the comradeship and honesty of fellow sufferers. On his more positive days, he thought about becoming a nurse. He was fed up with teaching, writing, and publishing, in fact with all intellectual pursuits. He wanted to do simple things like deliver cups of coffee, chop vegetables, or clean toilets.

As always, I felt close to Paul, even as I worried about him. And, as always, I, a therapist with a Ph.D. in clinical psychology, felt utterly helpless. And though Paul and I were writers, we couldn't find the words to make his life work for him. When I said goodbye the next morning, I suspected we would never meet again.

I would imagine that all of Paul's friends have pondered how they might have saved him. I've thought, "Maybe if I had stayed in better touch? Maybe if Jim and I had offered to let him live with us for awhile? Or if I had given him some books on Buddhism, or Jim had offered to teach him guitar?"

But what I really think is this—Paul's death by suicide was woven into his life from the beginning. Along with his wondrous joy, he contained black hopelessness. He was born wide-open to the world, a world filled with death and despair as well as beauty. Paul faced things alone. He craved respect, tenderness, and understanding, but he could not accept them. He could not be comforted or reassured. For all his brilliance, he was never able to comprehend how much we all loved him.

Work Cited

Gruchow, Paul. *The Necessity of Empty Places*. New York: St. Martin's Press, 1988.

Dr. Mary Pipher is the author of seven books including *Reviving Ophelia, The Shelter of Each Other* and *Another Country*. Her latest book is *Writing to Change the World*. She is also a clinical psychologist in Lincoln, Nebraska.

Letter from Iceland

Bill Holm

Introduction

A few years have now passed since Paul Gruchow's untimely departure from the planet—and as he might himself have thought, even said, the planet has seldom had more use for his wisdom. Paul grew fiercer as he aged, the sensitive natural historian growing into the excoriator of morons and rascals—a nice melding of Jonathan Swift and the prophet Jeremiah. I heard chunks of that evolving voice in *Grass Roots*, the last book published under his eye, but I heard it even louder in his public addresses—usually small savage essays delivered to audiences that had gathered to be cheered and flattered only to find themselves listening to a sort of intellectual whirlwind. He grew, in addition, more darkly funny as he aged, seeming to lose confidence in the ability of humans to think. Like Pagliacci, he laughed through his tears at the human race.

But now we are without that voice. Those of us who knew him well still hear it in our inner ear—particularly writers. When the subject of nature came into my work, I turned into Emerson, who had ideas but didn't know one tree from another. Emerson needed Thoreau, who knew everything he didn't know to keep him from declaring his foolishness in public. I am not the only writer in his circle and of his generation to have needed Paul Gruchow. How many chunks of pure ignorance about the facts of nature he amputated from my prose! Unfortunately, he left a sufficient amount of my ignorance, to which I had very likely become irrationally attached. I miss his clear eye.

In the world of books, I did better—but on more than one occasion, Paul astonished me by the enormous library he had filed

The Grace of Grass & Water

away inside his head, and digested into ideas and perceptions. I've only met a few that matched him in the scope and intensity of his reading. One night he lectured me on Shostakovich, singing aloud all the themes he'd been fetched by in a symphony he'd just heard. Music might have been the only subject where I knew more than Paul, but after that night, I wasn't so sure.

Last summer, I was asked for an essay for a magazine in Minnesota, *Blue Roads*. Since I spend three summer months in north Iceland, writing and staring out my front window at the Arctic Ocean, a ridge of big mountains, and a huge congregation of sea birds, I thought I'd imitate Auden and Isherwood's wonderful old book, *Letters from Iceland*. Nature, the environment—and the assaults on its integrity by greed, ignorance, and bureaucratic conniving —are at the essay's heart. A young Icelandic writer has decided to continue Paul's necessary work for his own country, and he comes into it, too. I tried to hear my old friend's voice while I was writing it, so I sent it not only to American readers but to any plane of astral ether where he might find himself at the moment. *Salúd*, Paul Gruchow of Rosewood Township, the Universe. We needed your voice in Iceland, as in western Minnesota, our mutual home, as in America, which grows steadily more dangerous and foolish without enough of you around to correct it.

Letter from Iceland

A letter from Iceland? To American readers? What grand precedent! Janet Flanner from Paris, Martha Gellhorn from

China or Havana, Martin Luther King from Birmingham Jail, Auden and Isherwood from the same Iceland, but to an audience in 1937 waiting poised but helpless for the start of WW II. Well, in America we wait no more. If we are anxious about war—if the spectre unsettles our sleep—we start a new one somewhere over something. Thus, we feel better. Waiting is hard business for the delicate psyche that services our oversized national body. Better to humor fear than endure or fathom it. So this will be a letter from behind a west-facing window in North Iceland on June 8, 2006 to an America solidly at war. That window is in my small house in a fishing village of almost 200, an historic Viking trading harbor now living out a mostly somnolent old age. The window looks west over eight miles of fjord that opens north to the Arctic Ocean. It faces a 3,500-foot mountain, Tindastoll, that rises almost sheer from the sea. I write behind a window because this morning (I begin at 5:00 am) a fierce, chilly wind blows from the west, driving big noisy breakers onto the gravel spit just 100 feet away. Beyond Tindastoll and the riled-up sea, if I keep looking straight west and follow strict latitude lines, I'm eyeball to eyeball with my fellow citizens 50 or 60 miles north of Fairbanks, Alaska—on the other far side of the planet. Since there are not many of you there, I'll cock my view a little south, missing Canada, to catch the sight and attention of more of you.

What's the news in Iceland? The usual in a 21st-century European democracy: a new prime minister, a weaker kronur, endangered halibut stocks, a depopulated countryside and a burgeoning Reykjavík metro, a higher gas tax, worries over new non-Western immigrants, population approaching 300,000 … 300,000?! How dare a country exist and claim independence with

79

a population smaller than St. Paul and a few of its suburbs? Yet here it is: all the apparatus of a prosperous modern nation-state, sans army (until this year, NATO and the U.S. provided Iceland's defense; now they're on the way out). Maybe Iceland will have to rely on the sea, isolation, long winters, and the absence of oil, gold, or diamonds to protect it from whatever the threats are— terrorists, guerrillas, fundamentalists—hardly a communist in the woodpile anywhere these days.

The local—Hofsós—news, like all local news, is mixed. The juiciest stories never make the papers. For most of its long history, Hofsós depended on fishing for its jobs, money, and reason for being. There's a small but very good harbor from whence a handful of small boats and one medium-sized trawler harvested cod, haddock, and halibut from the fjord. The herring, scallops, and probably the halibut were fished out in the recent past, but the fishing is still mostly good. The licensing system for selling fish devised by the Icelanders is, however, thoroughly crazy. To sell fish, you must own a "quota"; the more your quota, the more fish can be sold at market price. Quotas are wildly expensive, and you do not have to work a fishing boat to own them. They are bought and sold like stock, mostly to business sorts who have never set foot on a boat deck. Here, as in America, money follows money. The more you have, the more you get, the less disappears into the pockets of the unwashed working stiff. To make big profits, you need big trawlers that scrape the sea floor and decimate the fish stocks for their big-profit catches, thus big investments which require friendly relations with bankers and finally with mammoth conglomerates who understand money better than we do, whatever their taste in fish. Does this sound familiar to American citizens of farm states as they watch Cargill, ADM, and various banks and holding companies swallow American agriculture? Maybe there's more news for us in Hofsós than first meets the eye.

For several years now, I've watched fish caught a mile or two from the harbor loaded in trucks to sell in Reykjavík 200 miles south while fish from Reykjavík was trucked north to be salted down in the fish plant fifty feet up from the harbor. Capitalism and quotas in action to serve us all… but this year, much fish travels only the few yards uphill where it is dried and cured for "harðfiskur," an Icelandic delicacy best described as fish pemmican or jerky. It's wonderful stuff—tasty, healthy, low-calorie, good chewing exercise for your teeth. The Icelanders dip it into butter—generously—and I second their taste. Butter, at least in Iceland, is health food of a high order. Margarine, a cousin of ethanol, will certainly kill you. The reopened hardfish factory has meant more jobs and money in town. I recommend you ask your local grocer to stock it.

But the biggest local boat (not a huge one) is gone this year, along with its quota, felled by a bankruptcy. The local fellow who owned it had a reputation as a maritime crook, our neighborhood rascal. Rumors circulated of over-fishing (exceeding quota), fishing the wrong species, smuggling unregistered fish to the south for sale under the table, even harvesting illegal salmon from the fjord. Who knew what was true? Rascal gossip feeds the coffee chat in every village in the world, even New York. Last week, on an early June afternoon, about 30 mysterious cars and jeeps were parked next to the harbor. A big fishing trawler left carrying a crowd of passengers. The county rescue squad mysteriously appeared, and the county police (seldom seen!) patrolled the harbor and town all night. The rascal sold an illegal trip—no license, no life jackets—to climb one island in the fjord and have a boozy grill party on top of another, all the while in bankruptcy. Thus the trolling police. So far, this provided my most exciting night of window-watching in a month. It's a quiet place mostly (thank Buddha). In one way, the rascal is half a local hero. He provides entertaining tales (where do you imagine the sagas came from?), and he thumbs his nose at bureaucratic authority, getting mostly by with it. None of us love the cop, the tax collector, the bureaucrat. We love seeing an occasional fast trick get by them. It heartens us all.

But the large news that cleaves the Icelandic soul is the saga of aluminum smelting, because at its heart lies the question of what sort of country Iceland is to become. It is for Americans comparable to the question of the disastrous premeditated war we are waging in Iraq (and probably equally disastrously in Afghanistan). It causes us to look into our own mirrors and ask ourselves the hard question: what sort of country shall we now be? It will come as no surprise to Americans that Icelanders—almost 100%—like most of the rest of the planet at the moment, loathe the Bush gang and regard us as fools, bullies, villains, betrayers of our own great ideas. For what price have we (Icelanders, too) sold the good opinion of our own citizens—and the world?

Iceland, mostly because of poverty and isolation, missed the Renaissance, the Reformation (it arrived at sword-point from Denmark), the Enlightenment, the Industrial Revolution, indeed most of the last 800 years. It proceeded directly from the Middle Ages to the cell phone, the airplane, the Internet. Until 20 years ago, it had hardly a passable highway, still has no railroads (Icelanders who don't travel have never seen a train), no ghosts of obsolete mouldering factories. In fact, no factories at all, until an aluminum smelter arrived (via the Swiss) in 1969. Iceland had cheap electricity to offer (hydropower), and aluminum smelting eats vast amounts of it. The temptation to make "deals" with kindly corporate behemoths like Alcan and Alcoa proved irresistible to the Icelanders, and soon smelters will blossom all over the country, giving the volcanic wilderness a new look and feel. Americans should think long and hard on, for instance, Glen Canyon Dam before they begin chuckling at the naive Icelanders. We are of a piece in our avarice, we humans. To make electricity, you dam rivers, flood canyons, remodel nature to your own commercial ends. There's a lot of "nature" in Iceland: grand, bleak, eerie, uninhabited (probably uninhabitable) volcanic deserts, glacial detritus bullying its way to the sea through huge boggy marshes. That wilderness is home to wild reindeer, falcons, eagles, nesting grounds for a multitude of other birds, hideouts for outlaws. Astronauts trained for the moon landing here. It is like nowhere else on earth, and if the Icelanders keep selling it off to make beer cans for global conglomerates with souls and senses of honor the size of fleas, it will indeed exist nowhere at all except in photographs and memory. Like Glen Canyon.

The current bestseller in Iceland is a surprise: a book about, among other things, the still-in-process building of the giant dam at Karahnjukur in the wilds of east Iceland. It will create a forty-square-mile lake out of the black canyon of the Jökulsá (Glacier River) that will generate the mammoth amount of electricity needed to fuel the new aluminum smelter being built on an east coast fjord. The book, *Draumalandið—Sjálfhjálparbók handa hræddri þjóð* (*Dreamland—A Self Help Book for a Frightened*

The Grace of Grass & Water

Nation), is written in a spirit of informed anger by Andri Snær Magnason, an immensely talented young (33) writer, usually of poems, stories, plays and children's books. It has so far sold between 8,000 and 10,000 copies—and this to a population of under 300,000. I met a friend from Siglufjörður, a neighboring town, who had bought four copies, giving them all away after marking pertinent passages. He needed another for himself.

The title, *Draumalandið*, is a kind of joke. The song of that title is the most romantic song in an Icelandic singer's repertory. Icelanders weep at the sound of it. Dreamland is Iceland, home. So the Icelanders have sold their dreamland for a mess of pottage to the aluminum company—and not made a very good deal of it. They have put themselves at the mercy of Alcoa. Aluminum is now $3,000 a ton, but what rises falls. At $1,500 a ton, Alcoa will demand cheaper electricity or else close the smelter. Unemployment…discontent…bankruptcy…and the bill for the giant engineering project—tunnels, reservoirs, generators—will be left for the Icelandic taxpayer. Where indeed are the weapons of mass destruction? It will leave them a ruined, deflowered landscape to boot.

More smelters are in the works in various scenic places. Global capitalism and corporate butt-kissing for quick political and economic brownie points are a kind of addiction, needing its own 12-step program. Ask any co-op corn plant or grain elevator that's been bought out by Cargill or ADM. Ask your local Congressman if you can pry him off the golf course or away from the corporate junket.

Andri Snær's anger (Icelanders are always referred to by first names; the last is only a patronymic) comes not only from his love for nature and wilderness, and his mistrust of government, media and corporate gobbledygook, but also from his sense that this giant national undertaking took place without any real discussion by citizens, by no serious attempt to inform people. He writes a book, he says in an interview, because "'as soon as a newspaper article reaches one page in length, it is too long. A book can be over 300 pages and not be too long.… All education, whether it is history or something else, is contained in big units. Whereas the media, the news, everyone is trying to grab one headline, to fit in one press release… It is still too short to convey this reality'" (qtd. in Björnsson). Sounds like Rove-ian Washington spin to me. Remember the media buildup to Iraq, the shouts on the Fox News channel? Remember our leader's chant whenever he is asked a question that might require thought or real information? 9-11! 9-11! 9-11! So there!

Andri Snær thinks news is not a good way to learn about the world. "'People should just stop following the news. They should just stop accepting this form and denounce news. A bus rolls over into a ravine in India, what is the point? This tells us nothing. A bus falls into a ravine… If you were to do a little test on people concerning Iraq, what they now know about the country, and what they knew before, there is no new knowledge… People know nothing more about the culture, the literature, and the history. They know nothing more than that there have been bombings here and bombings there. They know nothing more about the forces behind the war, the thought behind it.… You are better off not knowing anything from the news about how the Iraq War is going, and read a book on the whole thing'" (qtd. in Björnsson). Icelandic media "has failed to critically assess the discussion of heavy-industrialization" (Björnsson). Media everywhere, dear Andri.

How Americans needed this young writer to sound an informed alarm—on so many issues confronting us. But that would require us to read whole books—in silence—and to think long, maybe contrary thoughts. Is it too much for us? Probably.

Icelanders remain the planet's most enthusiastic book buyers—and not only *Draumalandið*. As with us, romances, detective stories, diet and exercise books sell well, but also beautifully produced coffee table books about Iceland and its nature: birds, mountains, seacoast, fish, elegant photographs of deserted farms. The fancy books sell from $100-$300, ordinary books for $30-$100. Andri Snær's book, in paper, sells for about $40. The big publishing season comes in November for the Christmas book trade. Poets vie for the best-selling Christmas book of poems—maybe "5000 copies. This is roughly equivalent to selling five million copies of a book in America. Of poetry? Let's be serious now! Not even Frost or Billy Collins. Probably not even the Bible.

It's no surprise that I come here for three months a year to write and stare out the window. It's a good feeling for a writer to know that one's neighbors, despite their love of technological gadgets (more than one cell phone for each Icelander!), still love the feel of a book in their hands, the bite of type on a printed sheet. My travelling plans for the summer include visits to Halldor Laxness' and Gunnar Gunnarsson's houses, both now property of Iceland and national shrines, Glufrasteinn (Laxness) and Skriðuklaustur (Gunnarsson). These novelists are Iceland's most famous products of the 20th century, not hardfish, not beer cans, not rock bands or stars. For their legacy, they leave long shelves of books, still in print. Much Laxness is in print in English. I recommend him to you.

I want to end this sour letter on a cheerful note. It is now midnight on June 9, a warm still day, a few scudding clouds. Tindastoll, the big mountain across the fjord, has turned pink and lavender and has begun to glow. The sun has no intention of going down. The noisy Arctic terns are hunting in the incoming tide. A whimbrel just warbled from the grass under the window. A small fishing boat motored out of the harbor in pursuit of the decidedly unwily cod, leaving a pink wake in the now calm water. What Iceland reminds me is that while human beings seem to have lost all their marbles from fear and avarice, nature is still sane if we shut up, leave it alone, and look at it, seeing if some of its wisdom and loveliness might actually make us smarter and more humane. Henry Thoreau thought so. All we can do is hope for the best.

Work Cited

Sveinn Birkir Björnsson. "Welcome To My Nightmare: Discussing the Dreamland with Writer Andri Snær." *Grapevine* no. 6 (19 May 2006). Accessed 20 December, 2006 online at http://www.grapevine.is/default.aspx?show=paper&part=fullstory&id=1163

Bill Holm is the author of several books of essays and poetry, including *Coming Home Crazy: An Alphabet of China Essays*; *The Heart Can Be Filled Anywhere on Earth*; *Eccentric Islands: Travels Real and Imaginary*; *The Dead Get By with Everything*; and *Box Elder Bug Variations*. A winner of the Minnesota Book Award, Holm teaches at Southwest Minnesota State University in Marshall and spends his summers in Iceland, on the Arctic Circle.

The Grace of Grass & Water

Walking with Paul

Jim Heynen

In one of his essays, Paul Gruchow quoted himself as saying, "A walk on a prairie always puts me in a good mood" (*Worlds* 79).

A walk anywhere put Paul in a good mood, and to walk with him was to walk with a user-friendly encyclopedia of the natural world. He wasn't the kind of naturalist who would intimidate you with his knowledge by naming every leaf and mushroom that came into view, but I always felt pinched into opening my eyes because I knew he was seeing more than I was seeing. As a walking companion, he was a team player, someone who would let me set the pace and set the agenda for our conversations. Walking with Paul was like canoeing with Paul: he adjusted his stroke to whatever I was doing—and then praised me for my competence.

One of my first walks with Paul was through his garden when he lived in Northfield. His garden was more lush than fussy and seemed to have its own natural conversation with the earth. The garden was the first step on a pathway to his kitchen where he once cooked me *lefse*, that strange Norwegian dish that double-starches you with both potatoes and flour in one pancake. A walk through Paul's Northfield house included excursions through the jungle of his study and past memorabilia from his various adventures. The Northfield house, for example, had some grizzly-bear-damaged camping cookware hanging from the ceiling. Bear claws had perforated the lightweight pans when Paul and another companion had hung them "not quite high enough" while camping in grizzly territory.

Walking with Paul could be a way of connecting with his sense of humor. He knew that the natural world was packed with the essential elements of the comic—surprise and incongruity, to name a couple. Once, at the urging of an excited student, I walked with Paul to a nest of fledglings. The baby birds opened their beaks to the sound of our peering presence, and the student, awestruck, said, "Aren't they gorgeous?" We all did stand reverently before the lovely spectacle, but then I added, "Good eatin', too."

To the astonished bewilderment of the student, Paul burst into laughter. Of course, he knew nature's own perversities and surprises—its "tart reality." It was from Paul that I had learned that the sweet little critter of a chipmunk is in fact a nasty predator that can devour garter snakes and would as soon eat a robin as look at one. He knew that the natural world was not an escape from anything but often, instead, "a bracing call to realism."

The last time I saw Paul was when he was living alone on Park Point in Duluth, about a mile south of the famous drawbridge. It was a blustery, rainy day when I drove up to his rental house. By most people's standards, it was no day for a walk, but I suspected Paul would disagree. He admired in nature those plants and creatures that thrived through adversity. He thought humans were at their best, too, when they had to meet a challenge head-on, and I figured a good headwind might bring out the best in both of us.

Paul had warned me that the place where he lived on Park Point "wasn't much." He was right: it wasn't much. It was a narrow, inconspicuous little place, like a gardener's quarters, smaller than some trailer houses. The front door opened into the main room, which served as Paul's office, living room, and bedroom. The "bedroom" was a cot along one wall where he slept. The whole place felt bohemian to me, a setting for focused creative work. I asked him if he was writing. He told me that the very idea of writing repulsed him.

"Let's go for a walk," I said.

He didn't hesitate.

We set off, wearing hooded rain jackets. We started at the Maritime Museum and followed the boardwalk in the direction of downtown. The wind and rain got nastier, and when I looked over at Paul, I saw his smile.

"Bracing," he said.

Nobody else was walking out there that day, and Paul seemed to like the fact that we were distinguishing ourselves from all those ordinary folk who braced themselves against the weather by staying out of it.

"Perfect day for a walk," he said. Weather as adversary to our walking gave him a thrill. This was what being alive was all about.

When I noticed how the blustering winds were churning up a rusty root-beer color in the lake, I had a sudden recollection of the Wisconsin Dells and how a tour guide had explained that the root-beer color of the water was from tree roots upstream. With that fiber of knowledge, I asked Paul, "Is that color in the water there from tree roots?"

"No," he said, "that's volcanic ash that gets stirred up off the bottom now and then."

What followed was a succinct geology lesson about the history and formation of Lake Superior.

I was reminded of what a treasure we all had in the life and work of Paul Gruchow. I thought of another walk years before—this one with several people who had advanced degrees in the natural sciences. We were hiking the Lake Superior rocky shore near Wolf Ridge and looking at lichens. Paul didn't have a doctorate in anything, but the attentiveness of the scholars in the group told me who was the authority on lichens. Many of them asked Paul questions—and then listened earnestly to his answers.

Meanwhile, on that last walk I would ever take with Paul, with the wind pushing us from behind as we headed back in the direction of his house, we did talk about the pain in his life. He already had spent time in the psych ward and undergone electroshock treatment to challenge his chronic clinical depression. He was working part-time with mental patients in Duluth and told me he found the work comforting—and something that would keep him just balanced enough to divert his mind from suicidal thoughts.

"I'm supposed to call my doctors any time I have thoughts of suicide," he said, and chuckled at the irony of that, which I know he thought I would understand. I think I did: it was like telling you not to think about a sneeze that was forming in your sinuses.

When I told him how much I, and many other people, wanted him to remain in the world with us, he looked at me, not angrily, but with a rather puzzled look. He almost seemed to be sympathizing with me for not understanding a simple fact: whether to be alive or to be dead was no longer a significant distinction to him.

"Right now I want to live," he said, "because I'm having a good time walking and talking with you."

Work Cited

Paul Gruchow. *Worlds within a World: Reflections on Visits to Minnesota Scientific and Natural Area Preserves*. St. Paul: Minnesota Department of Natural Resources, 1999.

Jim Heynen is a native of rural northwest Iowa and now lives in St. Paul, Minnesota. His most recent collection of short stories, *The Boys' House*, was an "Editors' Choice" book of the year by *Booklist*, *The Bloomsbury Review*, and *Newsday*. His most recent novel is *Cosmos Coyote and William the Nice*. His 1997 novel, *Being Youngest*, was a Young Hoosier Book Award winner. Other recent books include *Standing Naked: New and Selected Poems* and *Fishing for Chickens: Stories about Rural Youth* (ed.). Earlier books include *The One-Room Schoolhouse* and the nonfiction book *One Hundred Over 100*. He has frequently been featured on National Public Radio reading his own stories and has been awarded National Endowment for the Arts Fellowships in both poetry and fiction.

The Grace of Grass & Water

Our Dead Colleague Who Did Not Suffer Cruelty Gladly

Carol Bly

Midwesterners tend to suppose that an author is lucky to come from a farm (best) or rural town (next best), and especially to come from Minnesota. How marvelous! Paul Gruchow's background, western Minnesota rural life, is the background of choice for oral histories. It's the background that makes memoir writing easy. Coming from a farm or coming from a little town squared off by fields of beans or corn means pleasant hours of writing for the low-key essayist or the nature-loving poet. All that hands-on feeling for nature and manual work! Actually, it is only half-marvelous.

Low-key rural essayists and poets can most accurately be said to *share* such feelings that sift around in their hearts. They love small tools. They love the surprising beauty of the moon's rising over the disked fields. They are commonly in love with the smell of whole-wheat bread being baked at home.

They especially love somewhat out-of-date tools. We all do. We lick it up about harnesses last borne by horses now long dead. Memoirists like to write and we like to read about the disk gangs scuffing along. And in the spring, we love how the huge planters scribe the fields and wheel their 180s at the headlands.

In the towns, we love to hear the chosen teenaged people shout to us the Gettysburg Address, which they have learned by heart for Memorial Day. For a moment we needn't think about thousands of American and other soldiers dying in useless wars. In their lyrical stories of Minnesota countryside life, share such pleasant comforts with us! We can generally count on slack authors not to say anything that makes us shout prayers like "O Christ, isn't there some way that *Homo sapiens* could be less cruel?"

Here is the half-conscious or wholly unconscious deal for comfy country writers: you writers keep describing the good old ways, or the fascinating lifestyle of animals and plants, and we will read your books. Do not remind us of the fact that our species, way too populous as it is, has partly wrecked and is further wrecking the beautiful spaces about it. We want to feel easy in our minds. If we can keep restful hearts by denying appalling news of over-population, we want to deny that news.

Two other griefs that beauty-loving readers don't want to think about are:

1. Cruelty to the helpless by governments—all the worse when perpetrated by our own government, and

2. The fact that human beings, ill-led by corporate interests, have doomed our planet, the only place where we can live. It's now doomed to heat up and likely kill us.

Some readers are not self-comfort addicts, though. Brave people read Jared Diamond and Richard Fortey and Bill Moyers just as, over a half-century ago, some comparatively brave people read Rachel Carson and Hannah Arendt and Martin Luther King, Jr.. Pain-avoiders, however, don't like such sharp flavors. They stick with aesthetics—such as descriptions of the beautiful if hard-working life of western Minnesota—Paul Gruchow's land. They don't want sages shouting a lot of morally terrifying news—news let's say, of cruel human practices.

Paul Gruchow was a moral genius. He was a sage—as well as what he was most known as, a charming nature writer. That so-called lucky rural background of his serves the nature writing but is a hard surround for young thinkers because they get no praise for rejecting simple love of beauty and nostalgia in favor of more intense feelings.

What is wrong with rural Minnesota life? Let me make some gross generalizations that I have noticed since 1955, when I first came to know and love farm life and farm-town life.

First, rural sociability is based on kidding. It distrusts all but cheery informality. It regards probing questions as something for adolescents to get over before we get any more irritated with them than we already are.

Since Midwest rural sociability depends upon kidding and a psychologically damaging informality, few of our writers put together inside themselves any serious philosophy of life at all. Hamlin Garland's ideas do not show up at rural Thanksgiving dinners. Garland especially hated the way canny business operators cheated innocent farmers. Garland, like Gruchow, liked nature and loved to think about it, but he had used his hours of solitude to grow up morally. So did Paul Gruchow. Both of these serious people grew to have less longing for mere beauty and more longing for an end to cruelty.

To write about cruelty, you must let feelings of fear and outrage whip across the core consciousness of your cortex. Garland did that. Gruchow did that. It means minutes and hours of not being happy, not feeling like kidding. Painful.

Psychological pain is a hard sell. You have to have some character to do it. For one thing, you do it alone. The other whist players grin at you. They don't suggest you shut up with all your gloom, because they are polite. Instead, they kid you.

Especially in our era, the 2000s, people living in the provinces are likely 90% uninterested in character as such, so courage—a dynamic of character, not a dynamic of loving beauty—gets very little made of it. Most people living in provincial places, here as in any country that still has anything you could call "provinces," are indifferent to any cruelty perpetrated by their country. Pain, anxiety or terror and much in between are always in the package of idealism. Different kinds of people hide from civic anxiety in different ways. The common countryside solution is to hide in practical projects—farming, say, even for decades, and shop projects until death. Homemaking, say. Or the kind of child-raising in which your goal for the kids is hygiene and citizenship, nothing so psychologically hefty as idealism.

Love of literature can be a gorgeous hiding place for educated people. Love of literature is very much like love of shop projects. Or love of natural beauty. Hitler's young protégés were great hikers in southern Germany and Switzerland. Natural-beauty lovers give statespeople a very free hand: you can put together a very powerful Reich full of beauty lovers. They will turn away from the sounds of screaming.

Practical people are tough parents for a young man or a young woman to survive if those young people want to become thinkers. Even the language they have heard from Midwestern women by the time they are beginning to think is so morally low-key that you can't conjure up an idea from it. The word "cruel" is rarely used. Instead we have "dumb." It's always something of a shock to hear someone tell about how someone else tortured an animal, for example, and then hear the listener say, "That is so dumb." Dumb says nothing morally. How can we dedicate any part of our lives to opposing cruelty if the people being cruel are regarded as only dumb, or goofy, or funny? No wonder Emily Dickinson so disliked informality.

Let's look at four words:

Dumb

Goofy

Funny

Putz

Those words say, "Never mind what you do or think; it's all low-key anyhow." They also warn us: you had better stay low-key yourself or we will bully you. We, your parents, may not be cultured enough or conscious enough to know that we are bullying you, but we will do it.

Two examples: What if you tell us that you only regret that you have but one life to give to your country? We will grin and say, "Oh for goofy." What if you tell us that the reason you fell behind the cavalcade of people was that you found the chance of a lifetime to talk to wise elders—sages? And then if you follow up with what in western Minnesota is called "smarting off" and ask us, "Do you not know that I must be about your Father's business?," we will get red in the face. "Don't get funny with us. If we are putzing around throughout the weekends of our lives, you had better putz around through the weekends of *your* life, too. Don't be dumb. Don't act funny."

Low-key language is an extraordinary tool of rural crowd control.

Therefore, it is hard for a genius to preserve throughout his or her childhood the inner flex and fire of disliking injustice—"injustice" being the legal cousin of the ethical word "cruelty."

A person gets lonely being the only intense one. For every Paul Gruchow who protects ethical intensity inside himself and decides to protect his own philosophy—philosophy meaning love for life which *connects* its millions of particulars (that's philosophy)—there are hundreds of nature lovers charmed in their heads with mere info about birds, plants, animals. In Minnesota, we have only a few dozen philosophically grown-up essayists and poets—Paul Gruchow, Tom Hennen, Bill Holm, Robert Bly, to name four. But we have hundreds and hundreds of low-key memoirists who are themselves enchanted with pieces of life. Their anecdotes make charming reading, too. Perhaps they got stuck in the culture of kidding. Perhaps no one told them this *concept*: that every member of *H. sapiens* has neurological potential for forming a philosophy of life.

Well—social workers and some clergy madly point the way out of kidding and into seriousness. They want us to have lived seriously before we die. Most of us don't listen to social work professionals because we don't know what social work is, and in any case we hate their jargon. We don't listen to religious professionals because most preachers in rural churches don't know any history or philosophy. We also hate *their* jargon. They bore us past tears. They are the robed and cassocked bloggers. Clergypeople, like advertising people, tend to keep discussions *rudimentary*. Their talk is sub-heroic.

Paul Gruchow was a hero in addition to being a gorgeous essayist. That is, he survived remarkable cruelty from both parents, and he survived the practical, non-contemplative life of a culture that clearly prefers kidding to moral grief. He became an author who could point out behavior that we should avoid. He found some *past* U.S. Senatorial behavior cruel, not just the present-day cruelty that smokes and drafts in our Senate. For example, not only did the United States rob German-American farmers of their land around Hastings, Nebraska, at the time of World War II, Paul wrote, but after the war, instead of returning that land to its owners, United States Senator George Norris converted it to a profitable deal for developers.

A priest in the Church of England once told me that some people simply never learn to dislike evil. Fr. Jack Putterill's remark was wasted on me. I took it quite calmly instead of gratefully because:

1. I had never heard the phrase "dislike cruelty" before, so it had no word recognition for me, and

2. I was untrained in ethics: I didn't know rule number one about any ethical statement, which is always ask the speaker to say more. "Listen, Fr. Jack," I should have said. "What's a specific example so I can see what you mean?" If there is anything even the least intelligent social workers teach, it is *empathic inquiry*—but at that time I had never heard of it.

If Paul Gruchow were alive still, I would ask him these questions:

"You weren't always a hater of cruelty: for a long time you seemed to be like other botanically minded writers—slogging along the field and meadow edges, telling us how some plants depend on one another and some are dead-set against one another and so on. What drove you to become a philosophical fellow?"

And I would ask him, "Listen, Paul, how did you do it? At great cost, of course, but will you explain the particular cost?"

These days, since 1986 for starters, and ever more now, neurologists pay all sorts of attention to this question: what makes someone who has been doing the usual for an artist (loving beauty) or does the usual for a descriptive scientist (studying various creatures' ontologies but not connecting their particulars with insight into how human beings behave on earth) contemplate the general, *connected* meaning of us?

An engaging neuroscientist, Antonio Damasio, is head of the Brain and Creativity Institute at the University of Southern California. How elegant that there should even be such an institute convened and run by disciplined, imaginative neuroscientists! Of course, neurologists have an advantage over us authors: they can now *see* with their elaborate imaging equipment the comparatively strong or weak firing in the brain in response to comparatively disparate stimuli—terror, horrible feelings of isolation, say, or cultural intake, hearing very elegant music versus mere clatter. In our lifetime, neuroscientists will be able to show us how it goes— how does a member of *H. sapiens* leave off the low-key shoulder-shrugging of someone not yet compassionate in order to take on the sentient joy of a philosopher?

I wish I had asked Paul these questions in his lifetime. I should have, because I had the sense at least to notice a huge difference between him and other people regarded as clinically depressed.

I was once in an English Department party given for the visiting lecturer in Northfield, Minnesota. There we all were, caving in to the Midwest courtesy of kidding, light humor, light cynicism, light nostalgia. Then Paul walked in. His eyes rather glittered, like eyes seen behind the grille of a knight's visor. Not friendly, not unfriendly. He was wonderfully alive. Without anything like grandstanding, he instantly changed the room's vapid cordiality into *ideas*. I should have asked him right then, "How did you get to be able to bear pain enough so you could philosophically tie all things in your life together? Was it perhaps that your parents were so mean that you learned to bear psychological pain?"

I didn't ask him because I am a Midwestern writer. I had my own languor. I had my own intellectual shambling.

At that time the women's movement was given great regard. One of its foremost tenets was that one needs a supportive family or a supportive group in order to develop one's own nature. A lie, alas.

When he was a boy, Paul's parents found he had rummaged in a drawer he was not allowed in. They placed an animal trap in that drawer to teach him a lesson. When next he rummaged in that drawer for something, the trap sprang and stung his fingers.

Second: One day, when Paul was a boy, he left home forever to live in the slough not far from the family farm. He spent an afternoon resting. He ate a garden-swiped supper. He climbed a favorite cottonwood in order to view the swamp nightlife. Presently he imagined himself dead and no one coming to find him. He slept in his quilt. Another day. No one came for him. Another night. At last he trudged home in time for breakfast. They had known where he was all the while, so they had not gone to him.

As with the mousetrap set deliberately in order to hurt him, it was a question of practicality. Practical people may well not ask children, "Why did you run away from home? Were you frightened or hurt or what?" Worse, however, which is more important than non-psychologists might suppose: practical people typically don't want to give their children a chance to speak *enthusiastically* about

107

how beautiful the moonrise was last night. Paul's parents didn't want to hear his feelings about natural beauty.

Third: Years passed. America entered the Vietnam War. Paul was opposed to it and spoke on Minnesota radio against it. His father heard the speech. When Paul got home the next day, his father stopped him at the door. He told Paul "coldly," Paul wrote, that he "was not welcome, that traitors were never welcome at his [the father's] house" (54).

This last unconscious cruelty of the father may appear to be in a different category from the other two, but, psychologically speaking, it is the same. In all three cases the parents do not stretch above their habitual practicality to act out of love. They obviously were not great readers of the Prodigal Son story.

The more important meaning is this: there have always been cold-hearted parents who are sometimes convivial. What is important is that if you experience cruelty—whether cruelty experienced in the home as Paul experienced it or cruelty vividly imagined because one has read some history—you have a chance to become a sage—that is, someone able to hang on to the curious idea that *love is better than practicality.*

I will finish by describing the funeral of someone who had nothing to do with Paul Gruchow but for the fact that she, too, was not praised for her noblest quality. In 2003, the University of Minnesota threw a gigantic memorial service for one of its most innovative and kind-hearted Minnesota professionals, Gisela Konopka. Gisa founded and directed the University of Minnesota's Konopoka Institute for Best Practices in Adolescent Health. The memorial service made no mention of the physical courage that Gisa had exercised in helping Jews and others get out of Nazi Germany.

She had been an undergraduate in the 1930s. Gisa and her boyfriend repeatedly risked arrest by the Gestapo. They were saving the lives of people they probably would never come to know. They got these strangers out of Germany. Gisa herself was finally caught and imprisoned by the Gestapo. A curious detail: the Gestapo kept Gisa enclosed in an upright, very narrow coffin-shaped box. She could neither sit nor lie down. Putting political prisoners in such upright boxes is a fairly classic torture. It has even been used quite recently by the United States at Guantanamo. It is said to be remarkably painful.

Over a dozen speakers came forward to praise Gisa at her memorial service. They praised her kindness with not just adolescent girls but with all manner of groups. They praised her loving empathy toward all kinds of people. They praised one of her standby virtues, her signature credo, which was her insisting that all people are equal.

Nobody mentioned her extraordinary courage with the Gestapo. If someone had told us about it, we would have been given a model of physical courage. Instead we got the usual easy rhetoric of memorials. The speakers chose Konopka's social-work graces to talk about. And what is wrong with that?

If you were an 18-year-old at that service, you would not learn from it that if you should eventually decide that you despise cruelty—let's say cruelty to prisoners or cruelty to civilians being bombed—here was help: here had lived Gisela Konopka to show you the way.

Therefore, in addition to our thinking of Paul Gruchow as a lyrical naturalist, let's stow in our memories this fact: Paul had a philosopher's classical hatred of cruelty. He was brought up in a Midwest culture that didn't give two cents' worth of support to that kind of hatred. He had to use his will to stick by a kind of courage that people around him didn't even vaguely respect.

Hard to do that in the rural Midwest. Paul was like a large sea beast needing to scrape its way out of the room-temperature shoals, to find and dive under the cold water that must be out there.

Work Cited

Paul Gruchow. *Grass Roots: The Universe of Home*. Minneapolis: Milkweed Editions, 1995.

Carol Bly is winner of the 2001 Minnesota Humanities Award for Literature, the University of Minnesota's Edelstein-Keller Distinguished Minnesota Author Award in 1998-99, and the Minnesota Women's Press Favorite Woman Author for 2000. She has an honorary degree from Northland College.

Her current book is *Beyond the Writers' Workshop: New Ways to Write Creative Nonfiction*, an Anchor Book from Random House. Other in-print work includes *My Lord Bag of Rice: New and Collected Stories*, published by Milkweed Editions in 2000; *An Adolescent's Christmas: 1944* from Afton Historical Society Press and *Changing the Bully Who Rules the World*, published by Milkweed in 1996. Recently reprinted work includes *Letters from the Country* (Univ. of Minnesota Press) and *The Passionate, Accurate Story* (Milkweed Editions).

The short story "My Lord Bag of Rice" was chosen for and published in the Pushcart 25th anniversary collection (2002).

Her forthcoming novel, *Shelter Half*, will be published by Holy Cow! Press in June, 2008.

A Gift of Sight

Mark Vinz

"In a dark time, the eye begins to see." —Theodore Roethke

As I look through my collection of Paul Gruchow books, I find
they're filled with markers—scraps of paper, Post-It notes, dog-
ears. So many passages I have wanted to come back to. So much in
those pages that made me stop and say, yes, that's it—no one else
has ever said it quite so well!

The markers indicate various subjects, of course, for Paul was
passionate about so many things, from the constantly threatened
state of the natural world in general to his vivid memories of the
ways he was shaped by the southwestern Minnesota farm where
he grew up. Indeed, I've always associated Paul most with specific
places. From the first time I read *Journal of a Prairie Year* or the
most aptly titled *The Necessity of Empty Places*, his eloquence
has always seemed to be *rooted*. What Paul taught me, perhaps
more than anything else, is the excitement of truly experiencing a
landscape—of being transformed by it—not only in his writing,
but also in his conversation, such as the afternoon we walked the
tract of native prairie near Felton, Minnesota, and he literally
danced around me, bursting with the names of things, crescendos
of information spanning biology, history, and geology, and always
underscored by an urgent sense of concern for what is being lost
in both the natural world and the rural culture that depends on
it. This 410-acre preserve (part of the few hundred acres of virgin
prairie that still remain in Minnesota) was indeed representative of
places usually taken for granted until experienced first-hand:

> A prairie is the most deceptive of landscapes. ... [It]
> offers no obvious point of reference, nothing for the
> wandering eye to seize upon as a starting point. As a

result, a prairie first impresses as empty, featureless, barren. (*Worlds* 75)

At the time, I was just beginning to appreciate the prairie—its overwhelming presence, its subtlety, beauty, diversity, and complexity—and I'll always remember how Paul's passionate eloquence showed me the way. But there was something more, too, something that continued to intrigue me the more I read Paul's writing, a central theme that involved the power of *seeing* itself:

I have had to practice the discipline of looking, have had to learn how to concentrate my attention on the visual symbols that reach my eyes…when my instinct is to walk blindly, to see everything indistinctly and indiscriminately.

We sometimes have the habit of seeing as children and then lose it, as we lose the gift of imagination; we lose at the same time the talent for seeing the world mythically rather than literally. (*Necessity* 266)

No matter what particular place Paul might be writing about, this essential and incredible capacity for wonder is one of the greatest gifts of his work (and if Paul Gruchow laments his *own* "blindness," where indeed does that leave the rest of us?). It's what I've come back to again and again in my own writing, for a long time now—what we see and what we don't see, what is all around us but which we take for granted, and what requires a very special kind of vision to reveal to us. This habit of seeing, as Paul called it, is something that evolves over a lifetime of caring and observing, reading and reflecting, and patiently seeking solitude—something he shares with poets and philosophers, and certainly with our greatest writers about places in the natural world, from Thoreau to Barry Lopez:

> Experiencing a landscape is an act of creativity. Like any creative vision, it cannot be forced or willed. No amount of busyness will produce it. It cannot be organized on a schedule, or happen by appointment. If you would experience a landscape, you must go alone into it and sit down somewhere quietly and wait for it to come in its own good time to you.... The solitude is necessary, the silence is necessary, the wait is necessary, and it is necessary that you yourself be empty, that you might be filled. (*Necessity* 146-47)

Paul's work is filled with respect for that awe-inspiring silence and solitude, indeed with poetry. He finds it in every landscape he enters, and, as we travel with him, we often share something that goes beyond words:

> The journey is indistinct from the traveler. As it is the instrument of awakening, so the traveler is aroused;
> what stirs is the inner voice of the artist. (*Travels* 20)

When this kind of awakening grows out of places that are often overlooked—such as prairies—is when I personally value Paul's work the most. To many of us, he'll always be essentially a prairie man. It's his writing about discovering his "own" place (one, as he says, that his education never encouraged him to be interested in) that leads me back again and again to "What the Prairie Teaches Us" in *Grass Roots: The Universe of Home*—as so much of Paul's writing, it is itself a kind of remarkable prose poem. It's revealed in the title of that book, too, in the linking of *home* and *universe*, a necessary starting point for all his journeys.

Now, as I reread passages from *Journal of a Prairie Year* and others of Paul's books that deal with prairies, I can't help feeling both a sense of loss for the "pale ghost of the world that once existed in this place" (*Journal* 65) and a tremendous gratitude to Paul for all he's been able to preserve in what he has shown us. I can't help thinking, too, that, like the prairie itself, Paul was a kind of enigma—wonderfully complex, slow to reveal himself, constantly changing, and possessing a profound sense of fragility and loss. Certainly, loss has been overwhelmingly present in his writing as he chronicled the destruction of both the natural environment and rural life as it once existed in this country (and our growing indifference to it), but it was unmistakably there in Paul, too. More than once when my wife Betsy and I would have him to our house for dinner during the years he taught at Concordia College in Moorhead, he'd spend the first part of the evening unburdening himself about the frustrations of not being able to reach his students, to somehow make them care about what they didn't know. Then, usually around 9:00, he'd excuse himself abruptly and head back to his office for a student conference. He'd cancelled all his regular class meeting times and was seeing all his students (at all hours) in individual tutorials, the only way he felt he could begin to help them. Unable to stop giving of himself, he was literally living in his office; unable to say no to friends or colleagues, the boards he served on, or anyone who asked him to give lectures or readings, he seemed to be erasing himself before our eyes. More than once he told me he'd probably never write again, though he thought that was all right, since he had other important things to keep him busy.

And then, at some point after we hadn't seen Paul for a few weeks, he astonished us with the news that he hadn't returned our calls because he'd checked himself into a local hospital's psych ward. If we'd been more observant, perhaps it wouldn't have come as such a devastating surprise—all we could do was remind Paul that we were always ready to listen, to help, however we could; characteristically, he responded that just knowing that would be enough.

The last semester Paul taught in Moorhead, when his wife Nancy had come to live with him, he seemed to regain a bit of his old demeanor. At least some of the franticness was gone from his eyes, and he was full of excitement about the property they'd bought near Two Harbors, Minnesota. He was ready to make the move and beginning to talk about writing again, too.

I don't remember seeing Paul again till the next year, when he and I and our wives had dinner together at a café overlooking Lake Superior. Paul seemed almost jovial that evening yet also somehow brittle, which was finally borne out by the card we received from Nancy that December. She and Paul were divorcing, and she was so frustrated about her helplessness to do anything about it; she'd become certain, too, that one day Paul was going to take his own life.

We tried every way we could to get in touch with Paul, but all to no avail. Though we'd hear about him occasionally from mutual friends, Paul remained lost to us until the day in January 2001 when I received an e-mail from him. I'd just sent him an obituary of the poet Roland Flint, whom Paul had known from his University of Minnesota days and greatly admired. He was

shocked at the news and thanked me for letting him know, and
then ended with the following paragraph:

> I had a strange dream the other night involving you
> and Betsy. Nancy and I had moved to a dismal town
> somewhere in the west, and you came to visit us. On the
> night you came, our house burned down, and since we
> had nothing else to do and nowhere else to go, we went
> out to eat at the bowling alley, the site of the town's only
> cafe. After dinner we asked for coffees. The place didn't
> serve coffee, but the waitress offered us certificates good
> for cups of coffee in Grinnell, Iowa. We left the cafe and
> set out on the thousand-mile journey to Grinnell for
> after-dinner coffees. That's where the dream ended. You
> and Freud can make of it what you will. Paul

I puzzled over that message for a long time, but found in it,
finally, something hauntingly familiar—from the echo of the
fire Paul accidentally set as a child and lamented all his life (as
he wrote in *Grass Roots*), to the decline of rural culture (the
only coffee-less café is in a bowling alley!), to the prairie person's
sense of space, the insignificance of miles. But there is also Paul's
unerring knack of finding something redeeming even in the dismal,
his cheerful willingness (or perhaps his restless need) to strike out
in new directions—and maybe a sense, too, of never being fulfilled.

Each time I read through Paul's work now, his dream somehow
seems to loom behind it, and the incredible zig-zag path of his
life. One particular sentence from an essay of Paul's called "The
Lost Habit of Seeing" has come to sum it up best for me: "We
wander as perpetual strangers through the world, and when some
odd moment of recognition finally comes, it serves to remind us

why we are so often and in so many ways lonely." That was indeed Paul—full of splendid epiphanies and so at home in the natural world, yet capable of being so directionless and unresolved at the same time. In *Grass Roots*, there's another passage that perhaps provides a kind of companion illumination:

> To inhabit a place means literally to have made it a habit, to have made it the custom and ordinary practice of our lives, to have learned how to wear a place like a familiar garment…. The word habit, in its now-dim original form, meant *to own*. We own places not because we possess the deeds to them, but because they have entered the continuum of our lives. What is strange to us—unfamiliar—can never be home. (6)

As a friend pointed out after reading a draft of this essay, perhaps the connection I've been exploring between Paul's life and his work is well captured in a line by the poet Theodore Roethke, another talented writer who struggled with depression: "In a dark time, the eye begins to see." And that's indeed an important part of what Paul Gruchow's work has reminded us of so often: in a culture that in so many ways discourages us from knowing or *seeing* either the natural world or those places that have become our homes, how necessary it is to have a friend who, in spite of the tragedies of his own life, will always be there to show us the path.

Works by Paul Gruchow Cited

Grass Roots: The Universe of Home. Minneapolis: Milkweed Editions, 1995.
Journal of a Prairie Year. Minneapolis: University of Minnesota Press, 1985.
"The Lost Habit of Seeing." *Minnesota Monthly*, October 1987.
The Necessity of Empty Places. New York: St. Martin's Press, 1988.

Travels in Canoe Country. Boston: Little, Brown, 1992.

Worlds within a World: Reflections on Visits to Minnesota Scientific and Natural Area Preserves. St. Paul: Minnesota Department of Natural Resources, 1999.

Mark Vinz has taught in the Minnesota State University Moorhead English Department since 1968, where he is currently Professor of English, as well as faculty advisor to *Red Weather* literary magazine and co-director of the Tom McGrath Visiting Writers Series. He is also the author of several books of poems, most recently *Long Distance*, as well as a number of published essays and short stories. He is also the co-editor, with Thom Tammaro, of two anthologies published by the University of Minnesota Press, *Inheriting the Land: Contemporary Voices from the Midwest* and *Imagining Home: Writing from the Midwest*, both of which won Minnesota Book Awards, as well as co-editor with Robert Alexander and C.W. Truesdale of *The Party Train: A Collection of North American Prose Poetry* and *The Talking of Hands*, both from New Rivers Press.

Escaped from Cultivation

Gary Deason

Paul and I had been hiking two days on Isle Royale, enough time to get our equilibrium after a rough crossing from Grand Portage, Minnesota. Since that first day, the weather had been glorious, although hotter than I expected for late May. I brought my camera—an old, heavy Konica with great lenses—to photograph wildflowers but found the showing to be somewhat disappointing. Surrounded by the slow-to-warm waters of Lake Superior, the island lagged weeks behind the mainland in spring color.

Paul grew weary of my frequent pauses to shoot yet another bloom about to open. We made a deal to meet at a designated campsite down the trail so he could exercise one of his few macho tendencies—to cover the miles—and I could dawdle, indulging my aesthetic side. It worked well for me, as he had camp established and dinner under way by the time I arrived. That evening, I found him stirring oxtail soup with a miniature wire whisk. I had only to eat, wash dishes, smoke a cigar, and share the day's thoughts with my good friend as we watched the sun set.

Although the wildflowers lagged, the diversity of vegetation did not disappoint. Here, as everywhere, vegetation followed topography which, in this instance, can only be described as "washboard." Formed 1.2 billion years ago when lava flowed from a crack in the Superior Basin and hardened into basalt, the island acquired its rippled surface when the Basin settled and tilted. High ridges and deep valleys formed along the length of the island with steep cliffs on the northwest side and gentle slopes on the southeast. Four major glaciers scoured the land, the last as recently as 10,000 years ago, deepening the sediment-laden valleys but leaving the hard basaltic ridges intact.

Crossing the width of the island is like riding a roller coaster through the ecological history of North America. On the coast, where lake waters keep summers cooler and winters milder than inland, white spruce and balsam fir thrive in the moist and shaded surroundings. Inland, where conditions are drier and hotter, sugar maple and birch dominate. In transition zones, a range of habitats appears from dense bogs with black spruce and white cedar to hillside meadows with jack pine and aspen. Temperatures vary as much as 30 degrees between the bogs below and the ridges above.

Even this immersion in diversity did not prepare me for what happened our third day out. We hiked together early that morning across the Greenstone Ridge, heading southwest from Lake Desor. Paul led, as usual, for he was the more experienced hiker. He had indulged my passion of canoeing the last few trips; now I returned the favor with this hike. I have never understood why otherwise reasonable people would heft a pack when they could float it, or sweat out a trail step-by-step when they could paddle almost effortlessly. Although inland canoeing is possible on Isle Royale, the fee to carry a boat on the ferry was too high. As we struggled across those hot barren rocks, however, I wondered if it might have been worth it.

Unexpectedly, Paul stopped and looked intently to his right. At first, I did not recognize what he was looking at, but then I saw it, or thought I did. Alone, with only a few strands of grasses nearby, rising prominently in an open field, stood what looked like, of all things, an apple tree. It stood proudly facing south, like an embattled Civil War soldier who had lost his regiment but refused to give up the fight. I hesitated to identify it, fearing I would show my ignorance thinking an apple tree could be growing wild in that severe climate, hammered by the vagaries of Lake Superior weather, in one of the nation's most remote national parks, now officially designated as a United Nations International Biosphere Reserve.

Paul uttered only three words. "Escaped from cultivation," he said. He stated it matter-of-factly, as though this technical botanical term were everyday parlance. I had not heard it before, but I have never forgotten it or the moment. Without voicing our thoughts, we stared at that tree, each considering how it had gotten there and the significance of our encountering it. Of course, the tree must have grown from an apple core tossed aside by an earlier hiker. Yet it clearly was flourishing and, judging from its height, had done so for years. The season was too early for fruit, but I know that tree delighted many unsuspecting hikers in late September.

The great American philosopher Ralph Waldo Emerson thought apples were native to North America, but philosophers rarely make good naturalists. Only the bitter and wrinkled crabapple is native. The wild apple, from which all domesticated varieties derive, originated in Alma-Ata in the mountains of Kazakhstan. Old World traders traveling from Asia brought the apples back to Europe, and, centuries later, European settlers brought the first cultivars to this continent, carrying them westward with settlement.

In the early 1800s, the legendary Johnny Appleseed (John Chapman, 1774-1845) distributed apple seeds and seedlings throughout the Ohio Valley. He planted orchards from seeds along the shores of rivers, several years ahead of waves of settlement, and then arranged for locals to manage the orchards and sell fruit to arriving settlers. Chapman found a ready market among settlers in large part because the rarity of sugar and grapes on the frontier made apples the fruit of choice for everything from sweetener to hard cider. Despite the do-gooder image of Johnny Appleseed, he was in fact a clever businessman who died with extensive real estate holdings and a fair amount of wealth (Pollan 3-58).

Some of the lore holds up, however, as Chapman had the rare ability to feel at home in the wilds and on the emerging edge of civilization. He befriended Indians and settlers alike, often sharing the proceeds of his sales with children, widows, and natives. His tireless efforts at disseminating apples on the frontier sustained the diversity of the American apple stock. Chapman refused to follow the standard practice of grafting, which produces only clones of the original. By planting seeds and seedlings, he took advantage of the rich diversity of the apple's genome and enabled natural variation to find those combinations that best fit American soil and climate conditions.

Although Johnny Appleseed never reached Minnesota, his efforts at preserving diversity improved the odds of that maverick tree on Isle Royale for surviving under the most unlikely conditions. I had tried to grow apples in Minnesota about 275 miles south of where Paul and I now stood. My experience duplicated that of many upper Midwest settlers, such as David Berry (who probably used grafted trees), when he wrote from Afton, Minnesota, in 1854, "Sir, in answer to your inquiries regarding apple trees, I beg to say on the 9th day of May, 1854, I set out 25 three-year-old trees. [They] came, I understood, from Iowa. None have escaped injury" (Gordon 23).

Minnesota settlers repeated these stories of frustration until John McIntosh in Dundas County, Ontario, discovered 20 wild apple seedlings on his farm. Soon he and his son established a nursery and distributed the famous McIntosh apple, which has become the leading cultivar in Wisconsin. I like to think, however, that the tree thriving under those extreme conditions on Isle Royale had the soul of a Viking and the valor of a Minnesotan. If so, chances are it was a Haralson, a tasty, hardy, and disease-resistant variety introduced in 1923 and now Minnesota's leading cultivar.

Origins aside, that apple tree held a lot of significance for Paul and me. Although we did not share our thoughts—we were guys, after all—we each identified with that tree and its bold venture into the wild. We too sought to escape domesticity, if only for awhile, now on Isle Royale and before that in the Boundary Waters Canoe Area Wilderness and in Rice County Park near Northfield where we lived. A long academic year of schedules, lectures, and meetings held the usual grind for two college professors who loved their work but also loved to get away from it. We were a bit envious of that tree, thriving in a place surrounded by beauty, unmanaged and uninterrupted. At that moment, we would like to have stayed and shared that tree's bold run on freedom.

"Escapism," my former wife called it, but she was only half right. Running from duties may be the "push" away from civilization, but there is also a "pull" toward wilderness, much more difficult to define and perhaps ultimately indefinable. I knew then, and I have often thought since, that the apple tree embodied that pull for us. Like it, my friend and I reached out beyond our ordinary lives, not only to escape but also to realize new possibilities. We

127

wanted to leave the world of predictability and enter a world where we did not know what was around the next bend, perhaps wolves downing a moose, or a stream reversing its flow, or a freak temperature shift. Of course, we never imagined a feral apple tree would be emblematic of our adventure.

For nearly four billion years, life has reached out, entered new environments, changed, and undergone extraordinary diversification across the globe. Isle Royale played a role in this stunning process. Widely divergent life forms gradually filled the niches of its varied topography, producing an island as diverse as any area of comparable size in the northern hemisphere. It is worth noting that this amazing diversification happened only after dispersion, after small populations of plants and animals reached out to new places and found conditions different from home yet, with luck, sufficiently accommodating to hang on until change and selection worked their magic.

Perhaps the primitive drive to reach out to new environments still manifests itself in the modern pull toward wilderness—the magnetic attraction to wild places that Paul and I shared and millions of others share, too. If so, the human genome might account for this tendency. Human chromosome number one (the largest chromosome) contains some 120 three-letter codes repeated nearly 100 times. Each of these codes specifies a unique amino acid, and the entire assemblage of codes specifies unique proteins. Every living organism exhibits the same sequence of codes, with almost no variation, as chromosome one. When the Last Universal Common Ancestor (LUCA) reached out beyond the primitive ooze toward land, perhaps those 120 codes played a role—and still play a role—in the search for new possibilities.

Some people are surprised (and some angry) to hear that chimpanzee chromosomes have the same genetic sequence as thirteen human chromosomes. This represents about 30,000 genes. Two chimp chromosomes are fused in humans, giving us 23 chromosomes instead of the chimp's 24. Overall, 98% of the human genome coincides with the genome of the chimpanzee. Genetically speaking, humans more closely resemble chimpanzees than do gorillas, which have a 97% coincidence (Ridley 16-28).

As recently as 3.6 million years ago, drought in Africa may have encouraged a small population of chimps to leave their dwindling forests and reach out across rapidly expanding grasslands, possibly seeking water. As mutation occurred, this population adjusted to their hotter, sunnier surroundings by losing hair, walking upright, and developing radiator veins in the scalp. They diversified their food sources to include meat, divided labor between males and females, increased their cranial size, and, surprisingly quickly, evolved through several stages into the remarkably successful species *Homo sapiens* (Ridley 31-35).

I would like to think that the escape from dwindling opportunities that led those chimps to new horizons continues in some deep genetic resonance between human beings, wild animals, and wild places. The great wilderness explorer and advocate John Muir thought so, too. "Going to the woods," Muir wrote, "is going home" (qtd. in Nash 128). To be sure, the pull of wilderness takes many forms, even unexpected ones. For the Harvard-educated schoolteacher Henry David Thoreau, himself experimenting with a sojourn in the woods, it took the form of savageness:

The Grace of Grass & Water

As I came home through the woods with my string of fish, trailing my pole, it being now quite dark, I caught a glimpse of a woodchuck stealing across my path, and felt a strange thrill of savage delight, and was strongly tempted to seize and devour him raw; except for that wildness that he represented. Once or twice, however, while I lived at the pond, I found myself ranging the woods, like a half-starved hound, with a strange abandonment, seeking some kind of venison which I might devour, and no morsel could have been too savage for me. (157)

While I have never felt the urge to devour wild animals raw, I have occasionally felt intense affinity with them. Late one winter night, about ten years ago, I sat in an easy chair, staring into the wood stove at my remote cabin in the Minnesota North Woods. I was feeling lonely after friends had left, and I stayed on to stretch out a few more days before another semester began. Chastising myself for becoming a couch potato, I strapped on snowshoes and found a near-full moon reflecting on fresh fallen snow. The breathtaking scene lifted my spirits instantly. I decided to trek around the lake, an outing I had never undertaken at night.

As I circumnavigated those frozen shores, I realized I was far from alone. One creature after another left tracks and probably waited now for me to pass before getting on with its excursions. A fresh set of tracks left by a snowshoe hare caught my imagination because it paralleled and occasionally crossed my own. I knew the hare and I had followed wildly divergent evolutionary paths to arrive at that lake, but I now imagined that we shared a similar history that brought us together in that place. The intersections of his path with mine symbolized our common ancestry long since forgotten, our solitary meanderings, and our common aspirations for warmth, food, and reproduction. A century earlier maybe I would have trapped that hare and eaten it, but with plenty of food at the cabin, I found in him an occasion for new reflections and insights.

At that moment, I fully realized that human beings are not ontologically distinct from other animals. Contrary to many Christian teachings, I saw that humans were not dominant or even pre-eminent over other forms of life (White 75-94). We are simply one successful species among many other species with which we share common ancestry. Reasoning capacity, inherent souls, and pontifical edicts notwithstanding, the hare symbolized what I already knew instinctively, what many Native American religions teach, and what Thoreau voiced during his own sojourn in the woods: "Shall I not have intelligence with the earth? Am I not partly leaves and vegetable mold myself?" Even rivulets of ice melting on an earthen bank reminded Thoreau of blood flowing through capillaries of the human body, symbolizing the onset of spring and renewal of life (103, 107).

Paul described an encounter similar to mine with the hare in *The Necessity of Empty Places*. This book was the first of his writings that I read. I liked it so much that I invited him to St. Olaf to give a public talk and lead a faculty workshop. As it turned out, he and his family were already planning to move from Worthington to Northfield, and so an invitation to speak turned into an invitation to teach and the opportunity to build a lasting friendship that influenced me, and still influences me, in immeasurable ways. In Chapter 18, after taking a wrong turn off the Continental Divide Trail, wandering lost for days, beset by loneliness and depression, Paul encountered a brook trout near Wall Lake and the Beartooth Plateau. The encounter renewed his spirits and offered a rare chance to find companionship with a very different species:

> The trout counted on being a shadow in the water, and I counted on seeming to be a shadow among the rocks. We were, for that brief moment, partners in a ruse. We played our parts automatically, without fear or conscious thought, reacting in our bones to the challenge of the moment….I did not know, in that moment, the difference between…the world of the trout and the world in which I lived and had breath. In that single pause on a rock above a channel in a mountain lake I had been invited by the gaze of a brook trout to join its universe. I have long sought such an invitation. (268)

The connectedness I felt to the hare and Paul to the trout resembled what a skilled hunter feels as he senses his prey. For a moment, I could see through the eyes of the hare, and Paul through the gaze of the trout. However briefly, we each became one with another species. "The hunter," Ortega y Gasset writes, "perceives all of his surroundings from the point of view of the animal" (142). Ancient hunters had to sense the entire landscape, the winds, the rivers and lakes, the habits of their prey and its food sources, if they were to find success and survive. Their physical and mental processes became one with the land and with their prey, to the degree that they could actually see the world from its perspective and anticipate its movements.

David Abram calls this type of holistic and immediate perception "participatory." Participatory perception, he argues, engages the entire body and its senses—sight, smell, taste, hearing, and touch. In *The Spell of the Sensuous*, Abram identifies participatory perception primarily with indigenous hunting-gathering cultures, especially those that continue to use the land today for survival. Unlike Western cultures that have progressively sheltered themselves from wild places and wild animals, active members of indigenous cultures have maintained the skill of perceiving holistically, sensing everything around them and participating in all that they perceive.

The hare incident notwithstanding, my own experience with holistic or kinesthetic perception has had less to do with biology and more to do with physics. Twenty-eight years of canoeing in the Quetico-Superior region of northern Minnesota and Ontario have taught me the lessons of basic physics in a totally experiential and participatory way. Paddling a solo canoe, one either learns these lessons quickly or finds oneself blown helpless and hapless against some distant shore.

Unlike tandem canoeing, the solo canoeist sits in the middle of the boat. On a still day, one stroke of the paddle deflects the canoe first in the front and then in the back. The paddler must continually adjust in both front and back with a "C" stroke in order to travel in a straight line, but with considerable loss of efficiency and power. On a windy day, both the bow and stern are exposed. Strategically placed packs ameliorate this vulnerability, usually the heavier in the stern and lighter in the bow. In addition, a sliding seat enables the paddler to adjust continually the distribution of his or her weight bow to stern.

The skilled canoeist takes advantage of all of these variables simultaneously, balancing the vectors of wind, weight, and strokes to travel in a straight line and does so more efficiently in a wind than without one. As the speed and angle of wind varies, the experienced paddler accomplishes all this without thinking, making adjustments with the sliding seat, leaning forward and backward, and paddling at different speeds. Solo canoeing in a stiff wind, in which success depends on skill and failure may have dire consequences, is the closest experience I have had to holistic participation in the forces of the world around me.

Of course, we all know that we participate in the vast theater of life, but we forget it when we regularly distance ourselves from the natural environment. The great cities that developed in Europe in the Middle Ages began to separate Western culture from nature. The Renaissance and voyages of exploration exposed Europeans once again to wild places and wild things. However, wilderness retained many of the negative connotations it had acquired through the centuries. The American wilderness contained life in unbelievable abundance and diversity, but early pilgrims associated the struggle to settle there with the challenges of the Israelites leaving Egypt and crossing inhospitable deserts. A leader of one of the early Puritan immigrations described the Atlantic coast of the New World as "a hideous and desolate wilderness full of wild beasts and wild men" (qtd. in Dubos 11).

Until urban life developed on the Atlantic coast, European settlers exhibited little appreciation of their surroundings or the Native Americans who immigrated there many centuries before them. European settlers began to appreciate the American wilderness only after Boston, New York, and Philadelphia grew to emulate the cities of the Old World. With the exception of John Muir (a Wisconsin farm boy), nineteenth-century explorers, artists, and writers were wealthy and well-educated urbanites who recognized an impoverishment in urban values that could be enriched by wilderness experiences. In very different ways, Wordsworth, Thoreau, Muir, the Hudson River artists, and many others reached out from cultured upbringings to find new possibilities for themselves and, through their writings, for American society.

Wild places, places full of new opportunities, have been a critical part of individual and societal development as civilization expands. In his famous essay "The Frontier in American History," Frederick Jackson Turner argued that the western frontier shaped the American character and defined our destiny. "Out of his [the American's] wilderness experience," Turner wrote, "out of the freedom of his opportunities, he fashioned a formula for social regeneration—the freedom of the individual to seek his own" (qtd. in Nash 146). The great tradition of American wilderness literature, shaped largely by urban-educated wanderers who ventured westward, portrays wild places as sources of redirection and renewal for weary citizens burdened by the trappings of urban life. Wild places offer prospects for redressing the imbalances of civilized life, either for an individual underwhelmed by predictability or a society overwhelmed by commercialism.

As Paul and I stared at that apple tree, we silently rehearsed the great themes of freedom, self-reliance, beauty, and spirituality articulated in our distinctively American literature. I had learned many of those themes the previous year as he and I taught *American Nature Writers* to eager St. Olaf College students

The Grace of Grass & Water

looking for understanding and justification of their own yearnings to abandon the classroom and wander through what remains of North America's wild places.

Those students always liked John Muir. He embodied vitality and adventure better than any other wilderness advocate. Growing up on a marginal farm with a strict father, Muir longed to escape to wild places, which, for him, offered solace, beauty, and spiritual renewal. An extraordinarily inventive young man, he left the University of Wisconsin before graduating to wander through parts of Canada, the Midwest, the Southeast, and California. He finally found a home in the sublime mountains of the Sierra Nevada range and Yosemite. (Coincidentally, later in life, Muir explored the glaciers of Alaska with financial support from an apple orchard that his wife tended back home!) A naturalist overflowing with enthusiasm for his subject, Muir wrote with a rare ability to bridge the natural sciences and humanities. His essays are at once scientific analyses and poetic rhapsodies, so enthused does he become with his subject or, more correctly, with the exciting adventures that pursuit of his subject offered.

Although Paul has been called "Minnesota's Thoreau," in some respects he resembled Muir more than Thoreau. His writings reveal great powers of observation and detailed scientific understanding, but also warm humanism. They exude his love of adventure and thrill of discovery. How often have his essays captivated us as he realizes his distracted pursuit of a subject has left him hopelessly lost or helplessly falling off a ledge with a full pack on his back into a pool of water? While adept in numerous ways, Paul had an absent-minded clumsiness that often got him into trouble, but also genuinely endeared him to us. Once on Alder

136

Lake in the BWCAW, while eagerly showing me the difference between sedges and grasses, he leaned out too far and flipped the boat over. As we both came up sputtering, he had the presence of mind to say, "At least I only do this in shallow water."

A true wilderness experience, then, is like visiting another culture. New possibilities await the traveler every day. He or she experiences a release from the ordinary in the form of new encounters, habits, and schedules. The longer the visitor remains immersed in the culture, the more he or she brings home. Experiences in wilderness, like experiences abroad, have a way of downsizing life to its essentials. One travels lightly and focuses only on what is important to see or do. Knowing time is limited, the savvy traveler manages time more carefully. There is a liberating feeling about focusing on essentials. It helps rid the mind and emotions of clutter so that life can be lived deliberately.

Sometimes, however, even good friends disagree over what is essential. I had been in the final steps of a divorce and staying at Paul's house when we decided that a long weekend in the Boundary Waters would be cathartic. We camped the first night on Pine Lake near the trail to Johnson Falls. Due to the heat, we put in early and had time to loll around camp. Paul soon spied a dragonfly molting. He called me over to watch this painstaking process unfold. It was fascinating, but after awhile nature called in another way, and I headed for the privy. As I walked back, I did a double take when I saw Paul waving goodbye to two attractive women who were just paddling away from our campsite. I could not remember a time in over a decade of canoeing the BWCAW that I had encountered a moment so promising, yet unpromising. I rushed to him and asked what was up. He said the women needed a place to stay, but he told them he was busy making sketches of a dragonfly and suggested they look elsewhere!

By focusing on essentials, the wilderness traveler, like the visitor abroad, brings back the lesson that one's own culture is largely convention. However, the conventions often take on new significance. Who hasn't renewed an appreciation of running water or reliable telephones or a home-cooked meal after returning from the woods or abroad? The differences between home and other cultures, not the similarities, teach us about the essentials of life and heighten our appreciation of the non-essentials. The contrasts provide new experiences and new insights, not the consistencies or uniformities. A global society with freeways through every city and McDonald's in every neighborhood does not have the potential of enriching the traveler in the same way as one that maintains the integrity of distinct cultures.

So it is with experiences of nature. Lavishly outfitted summer homes and national parks with RV stalls do not offer genuinely different experiences. They are hybrids of nature and culture, not heritage seeds pregnant with history and diversity. To learn from wilderness, we must maintain wild places distinct from our social conventions so that we can experience the contrasts and learn from them. Like paddling the solo canoe, the secret lies in balancing discrete forces, not in eliminating them. In this sense, we should side with Thoreau, not Jefferson. We should maintain some wild places near our communities, not surround them with fields and pastures or, worse, golf courses. Not only will the land remain healthier, but we will have greater opportunity to remain healthy by learning from diversity.

Wild places adjacent to cities or towns do not need to be large or spectacular. They only need to have some distinctive features and offer possibilities that are out of the ordinary. Rice County Park between Northfield and Faribault offered Paul and me numerous chances to discover new worlds near home. At the end of a workday or on a Saturday afternoon, we stole away to this lovely little piece of the planet, which a group of local residents had the foresight to protect. The Cannon River, which French explorers named "River of Canoes" due to its frequent use by Native Americans, flows through Rice County Park. It provides silent paddle access to parts of the park unknown to hikers. We were, in Thoreau's phrase, "charting our own cosmography."

On one such paddle, we stopped onshore for lunch. As we talked, Paul's gifted and practiced eye spotted a rare treasure. "Oh my," he exclaimed, "a dwarf lily." The Minnesota dwarf trout lily is the state's only endemic species and one of the rarest plants in the United States. I had never seen one before. For me, in that moment, a simple day trip turned into a once-in-a-lifetime event. We immediately began combing the area and found three colonies of dwarf lilies, more than even Paul had seen. It is entirely possible that no one else has ever seen those colonies, either before or since. I took pictures of them that remain a special memory of a special afternoon, an afternoon in which a shared discovery in a local nature area became a life-enriching experience for two would-be explorers.

Our cat, Bob, knows the value of wild places. Three years ago, he walked out of the woods and adopted us. Since then, Bob has led two lives, indulging in the best of both worlds. By day, he roams the forest, setting his sights on the local rodent population.

He tests all of the skills of the hunter—senses, speed, reflexes. He relives his genetic heritage by manifesting behaviors that have made felines an old and successful evolutionary line. At night, or most nights, Bob relaxes at home. He has a can of food (more eagerly if the hunt wasn't successful) and curls up on the rug or in my wife's lap. Having hunted by day, Bob becomes a family man at night and, in my imagination, enjoys relaxing with his adopted pride while we read or watch a video. Bob lives a life we all should envy. His home is adjacent to his woods.

Animals like Bob, and humans like us, have a distinct advantage over plants. We can move. By moving, we reach out to new places and find new possibilities. Plants reach out, of course, by scattering their seed, but the individual plant remains in place. By a hiker's hand, the apple seed on Isle Royale took a leap, but the mature tree remains fixed. It cannot choose now to try out the orchard. It must survive where it is or die. I have not been back to learn its fate; sometimes I imagine it has died, but usually I hold out hope that it still surprises unsuspecting hikers.

If that tree could choose, I like to think it would choose the wild, even with imminent death, rather than living out its years in an orchard. I know Bob would choose the woods. As much as he enjoys a dry home and an occasional can of grilled tuna, he howls like a jilted suitor when he cannot go outside. Trapped inside, his life shrinks to a few hundred square feet, and his prospects for new encounters and adventures shrink proportionally. He tries to make the most of a bad deal by exploring every room, but the territory is familiar and the discoveries are few. Eventually he gives up and goes to sleep.

After Paul's illness held him firmly in its grip, I invited him to my cabin where we had had so many good times. I invited him to walk with me on a new section of the Superior Hiking Trail. I invited him to move with me to Flagstaff, Arizona, and explore the wonders of the Grand Canyon and ancient Southwest cultures. He politely declined these invitations, saying that he needed to stay near his doctors and near the medical and social service systems in Duluth. His world had shrunk, and he needed, understandably, to focus on himself and try to hold the pieces together. In his own essay about Isle Royale, Paul wrote:

> At the extreme, in mental illness, all of a person's available energy is required to keep the pieces of the broken self together, leaving none for relationships with other living beings.…One important reason for preserving wilderness remnants like Isle Royale in a world ever more intensely exploited by burgeoning humanity is that such places remind us that human-centeredness is a delusion. They keep us quite literally sane. (*Boundary Waters* 174)

Shortly after we arrived in Arizona, I learned that Paul had ended his life. I have often asked myself if I should have tried harder to lure him back to the wild places that he loved so dearly and that held such significance for him. I have often asked what I would do given the shrinking world of possibilities that he faced. Perhaps I would make the same decision as he. Perhaps it is so with humans bound by illness and medications and systems serving mental health, who face living in chains or reaching out to new unknowns. Perhaps they allow those ancient wild genes to find expression in a final escape from cultivation.

Note: I want to thank my friend and colleague Gary Paul Nabhan for his careful reading of this essay and his helpful suggestions.

Works Cited

Abram, David. *The Spell of the Sensuous: Perception and Language in a More-Than-Human World*. New York: Random House, 1996.

Dubos, René. *The Wooing of the Earth: New Perspectives on Man's Use of Nature*. New York: Charles Scribner's Sons, 1980.

Gasset, José Ortega y. *Meditations on Hunting*. Tr. Howard B. Wescott. New York: Charles Scribner's Sons, 1972.

Gordon, Don. *Growing Fruit in the Upper Midwest*. Minneapolis: University of Minnesota Press, 1991.

Gruchow, Paul. *Boundary Waters: The Grace of the Wild*. Minneapolis: Milkweed Editions, 1997.

—. *The Necessity of Empty Places*. New York: St. Martin's Press, 1988.

Nash, Roderick. *Wilderness and the American Mind*. New Haven: Yale University Press, 1967.

Pollan, Michael. *The Botany of Desire: A Plant's-Eye View of the World*. New York: Random House, 2001.

Ridley, Matt. *Genome: The Autobiography of Species in 23 Chapters*. New York: Perennial/Harper Collins, 2000.

Thoreau, Henry David. *Walden, or Life in the Woods*. New York: Harper & Row, 1965.

White, Jr., Lynn. *Dynamo and Virgin Reconsidered: Essays in the Dynamism of Western Culture*. Cambridge MA: MIT Press, 1968.

Dr. Gary Deason serves as Deputy Director of the Center for Sustainable Environments at Northern Arizona University (NAU) in Flagstaff. He works with NAU, the Flagstaff community, and the State of Arizona to advance more sustainable practices, policies, and technologies associated with energy, water, waste, transportation, and community design and development. Deason directs the NAU campus sustainability program, coordinates a campus program for environmental research, and sits on the Governor's Solar Energy Advisory Council.

Prior to NAU, Deason served as President of Wolf Ridge Environmental Learning Center in northeastern Minnesota, the nation's second-largest center devoted wholly to environmental education. As a founder and member of the St. Olaf College Environmental Studies program for 15 years, he taught courses related to land, water, air, wildlife and wilderness. At St. Olaf, Deason started a program that helped over 300 school districts throughout Minnesota develop school nature areas and trained over 1000 teachers in environmental education.

The Treasure

Bob Artley

drawing © Bob Artley

In one of Paul Gruchow's letters to me, he apologized for being "so elusive" (Paul was hard to contact while he was battling depression). He made the following comment: "I'm convinced that some treasure lies beyond this darkness, and I hope you'll be patient with me until I get to it."

Surely, I feel, he must have reached that "treasure" by now. And my hope is that I will sometime be able to join my dear friend as he explores the "treasure beyond this darkness." As I get to the age when my sense of mortality becomes ever-present in my day-to-day consciousness, I approach this phenomenon not with a sense of morbidity, but rather speculation at just what the next phase of existence will be like.

My wife, Margaret, and I speak of this next phase quite often, not with dread, but only with the expressed hope that one of us won't be left alone for very long. We speak of when we will again be with loved ones who have already made the transmutation. Margaret's first marriage of forty-eight years to Bill and my first marriage of nearly fifty years to Ginny provided each of us with much happiness. So we are both anticipating seeing our former mates again. This condition of looking forward and once again being with our loved ones, our family and friends, provides that phenomenon we call death with a pleasant aspect.

For me, after first reuniting with family members and friends who have preceded me into this new existence, I want to engage my old friend Paul to be my guide into the "treasure" of which he spoke. For while he was here on Earth, he did a superb job of helping me and many others see, understand, and appreciate the wondrous natural world we have around us.

I feel certain that, in the extension of life beyond what we call death, there is a natural environment that is the ultimate realization of what we had, in its pristine state, here on Earth, before humankind started exploiting it in the name of "progress." In this ultimate environment, this Heaven, or whatever we choose to call the place where our soul (the essence of who we are) resides, I can think of no one I'd rather have accompany me in exploring this "treasure" than Paul Gruchow.

Paul, because of his illness, was able to visit Margaret and me only briefly when we spent our summers in Iowa. We always hoped for a longer visit, so whenever we got back to Florida for our winter stay, we would plan for him to visit us. But Paul's poor health always intervened, and his visits had to be canceled.

This was a disappointment for all of us, for there are many areas in Florida that I am sure Paul would have found interesting. There are unspoiled areas such as forests where Southern Oaks, draped with Spanish moss and some of them very large, are ancient inhabitants. And there are many different kinds of palm trees as well as ground-cover species. There are marshes with varied native denizens. And of course there are expanses of prairie which are so different from those Paul knew and described so well in his writing.

In addition to the flora of Florida, Paul would have found many of the aspects of the state's wilderness areas worthy of his study. I can imagine how enthusiastically Paul would have delved into a study of the Everglades, that subtropical swamp encompassing about 1700 square miles of southern Florida. The Everglades, according to the American Heritage Dictionary, lies on limestone plateau. This great expanse of swamp (sometimes referred to as a "river of grass") has been designated a federal preserve in order to protect the abundant wildlife and tropical plants found there.

I would have liked so much to have accompanied Paul as he explored the wildness of this state. He could have taught me much about the natural environment of Margaret's and my adopted state, just as he did about the states of Iowa and Minnesota, showing us the "treasure" we had all around us there.

Thank you, Paul. I'll see you later.

Bob Artley was born in Hampton, Iowa, on July 1, 1917, on the family farm established by his grandfather in 1877. Artley began drawing as a boy and was encouraged by his parents, teachers, and *The Des Moines Register* and *Tribune's* acclaimed cartoonist, Ding Darling. He attended country schools through the eighth grade. After graduating from high school, he attended Grinnell College and studied art until he was drafted into the US Army in 1941. While serving in the Armed Forces, he met and married a WAC medical technician, Virginia (Ginny) Moore. After the war, the young couple returned to the farm, built a house, and farmed with Bob's father for a few years. Bob then enrolled at the University of Iowa, where he studied art and graduated in 1951.

Artley's career as an editorial cartoonist began with the *Des Moines Tribune* and continued at the *Worthington Daily Globe* (Minnesota), where he launched his syndicated cartoon series, *Memories of a Former Kid*, which was the genesis of his first book.

Additional Ice Cube Press Books

Letters To A Young Iowan: Good Sense from the Good Folks of Iowa for Young People Everywhere, Zachary Michael Jack, editor, 1-888160-21-7, $19.95
Featuring contributions by over 100 Iowans on what a young Iowan needs to know to grow up well in the Hawkeye State (or anywhere, for that matter). Editor Zachary Michael Jack has brought together a once-in-a-lifetime who's who of over one hundred contemporary Iowans, including Dan Gable, Robert Ray, Marvin Bell, Dean Borg, Jim Leach, Christie Vilsack, Mary Swander and many more! Each offers advice and good common sense to young people, ranging from the mundane—how to walk a gravel road—to the comically profane.

Firefly in the Night: A Son of the Middle West, Patrick Irelan
1-888160-20-9, $16.95
A candid and humorous story of a life repeatedly interrupted by emergencies. Irelan tells his story the only way he can, with more humor than the events recorded might seem to require. As a child he learned a set of values from his parents and other elders. He has lived his life according to those values, but with occasional revisions that have allowed him to survive the absurdities of modern times.

River East, River West: Iowa's Natural Borders
1-888160-24-1 , $12.95
Writings by David Hamilton, John Price, Gary Holthaus, Lisa Knopp, and Robert Wolf, with "creekography" by Ethan Hirsh, on the meanings, history, folklore, nature and ideas of the two rivers bordering our state. As this book shows, the Mississippi and Missouri Rivers are much more than the water that flows in them.

Prairie Weather
1-888160-17-9, $10
Iowa is at the crossroads of the elements—just above our heads whirl other-worldly tornadoes, and summers bring bone-drying droughts, while winter brings walls of snow. In our region of four seasons, we

can learn much from our weather. Writing and photographs by Jim Heynen, Mary Swander, Deb Marquart, Amy Kolen, Ron Sandvik, Mark Petrick, Ethan Hirsh, Robert Sayre, Thomas Dean, Patrick Irelan, Michael Harker, Scott Cawelti, and a foreword by Denny Frary.

Living With Topsoil: Tending Our Land
1-888160-99-3, $9.95

A full-fledged exploration via Iowa's finest authors into living with our state's world-famous topsoil. New and valuable writing by Mary Swander, Connie Mutel, Michael Carey, Patrick Irelan, Thomas Dean, Larry Stone and Tim Fay, and an introduction by Steve Semken. Jose Ortega y Gassett once wrote, "Tell me where you live and I'll tell you who you are." You'll find out what it means to live in the land of amazing topsoil once you read this book.

The Good Earth: Three Poets of the Prairie
1-888160-09-8, $9.95

Surprisingly, there is a strong tradition of prairie poetry in Iowa. This work features the prairie-based works of legendary poets Paul Engle, James Hearst and William Stafford, examined, respectively, by Robert Dana, Denise Low and Scott Cawelti, with a foreword by Iowa farm poet Michael Carey. In the tradition of place-based stories, this book finds connections between spirit and place. As if that isn't amazing enough, this collection also includes one previously unpublished poem by Iowa's famed Writers' Workshop director Paul Engle.

Prairie Roots: Call of the Wild
1-888160-12-8, $10.95

An exploration into the meanings of the wild in the Midwest, featuring one of the last published essays of the late Minnesota author Paul Gruchow. This intriguing collection explores other facets of Iowa and the prairie landscape: a fascinating examination of landscape art by Joni Kinsey, the results of the "grid" system laid upon our land by Robert Sayre, poetry by Mary Swander, the flight and call of geese by Thomas Dean and a discovery of giant worms by Steve Semken. Photography by Rev. Howard Vrankin.

Words of a Prairie Alchemist, Denise Low
(Poet Laureate, State of Kansas)
1-888160-18-7, $11.95
The Great Plains of the North American continent have dramatic seasons, intense colors, alchemical thunderstorms, and epic winters. Denise Low has emerged as one of the most trusted writers of this region. With a balance of drama and finesse, she describes the juncture between the natural world and the human realm of literature.

Ordering Information:
Books can be ordered directly from our web site at
www.icecubepress.com
or by mail (check/money order) by sending to
Ice Cube Press
205 N Front St.
North Liberty, Iowa 52317-9302

(shipping $1.50 first book, .25¢ each additional)

The Ice Cube Press began publishing in 1993 to focus on how to
best live with the natural world and understand how people can
best live together in the community they inhabit. Since this time,
we've been recognized by a number of well-known writers, including
Gary Snyder, Gene Logsdon, Wes Jackson, Annie Dillard, Kathleen
Norris, and Barry Lopez. We've published a number of well-known
authors as well, including Mary Swander, Jim Heynen, Stephanie
Mills, Bill McKibben, Ted Kooser and Paul Gruchow. Check out
our books on our web site, with booksellers, or at museum shops,
then discover why we are dedicated to "hearing the other side."

Ice Cube Press
205 N Front Street
North Liberty, Iowa 52317-9302
p 319/626-2055 f 413/451-0223
steve@icecubepress.com
www.icecubepress.com

& to the coolest of the cool
my all-time favorite gals:
Fenna Marie & Laura Lee

Elegy For Paul Gruchow

You've been gone one week
wandering a remnant of prairie
crossing the still frozen lakes
of Minnesota
your snow shoe tracks disappearing
and no one can find you.
This morning I woke in pain
needing to hear your voice.
You aren't coming back, old friend.
There is no return address
no way to reach you with a question:
How will we survive a time
in which even one brave as you
could not stop his hands
from shaking at a lectern?
I miss most your laughter—
how you held back nothing
your whole body convulsing
when we watched that movie
about the psychiatrist
driven mad by his patient—
how you writhed on the floor
in pure cathartic delight.
Today there are no words from you
but I will go on listening still,
this large silence your eloquence now.
    —Louis Martinelli

A portion of the profits from this book will be contributed to the

Paul Gruchow Foundation
*"There is no death so final as
the death of a memory."*
—Paul Gruchow

Mission Statement:
To foster awareness of the
relationship between nature,
creativity, community and
mental health.

Objectives:
1. To make literary work by and
about Paul Gruchow available
to a wider audience.
2. To create a website and
newsletter explaining the work
of the foundation and publishing
writing relevant to its mission.
3. To sponsor an artist in
residence program.
4. To facilitate retreats for
individuals and groups committed
to exploring the relationship
between nature, creativity,
community and mental health.

Executive Director: Louis Martinelli
Board of Directors Chairperson:
Mary Doucette
The Paul Gruchow Foundation
33246 Highway 56 Blvd.
Dennison, Minnesota 55018
lamartinelli@msn.com